A SUMMER WITH SWAMIJI

Discourses and Satsang with
Paramhans Swami Maheshwarananda

A SUMMER
WITH SWAMIJI

Given at the summer retreats in
Austria, Hungary and Czech Republic
July and August 1992

Cover Design:
Matěj Hlaváček (Yogapuri)

ISBN 978-3-903362-07-9 Paperback
ISBN 978-3-903362-08-6 eBook

"God's well is never dry"

Paramhans Swami Maheshwarananda

Content

Foreword

For one blessed summer, we had the great good fortune of being able to accompany our Master, Paramhans Swami Maheshwarananda Ji, to his retreats in Austria, Hungary and what was then known as Czechoslovakia. Blessed also is the time we have spent in transcribing his wonderful discourses and *satsangs*, so that all those friends who were unable to be there also have the opportunity of sharing in Swamiji's words of wisdom and truth.

SATSANG means a coming together in the service of truth and the divine. SATSANG is the ship that can carry us across the dark ocean of our earthly miseries to the enlightened shores of realisation of our true Self.

Swamiji's talks masterfully demonstrate the connection between the four different paths of Yoga: BHAKTI, KARMA, RAJA and GYANA YOGA.

BHAKTI YOGA is spiritual love and devotion to God – the path of the heart. KARMA YOGA means selfless action and helping others. RAJA YOGA is the "Royal Yoga", the path of practice and meditation. GYANA YOGA means knowledge of the Highest Truth, and is the path of realisation and discernment between the eternal, divine reality and the transitory unreality.

In these talks Swamiji clearly and practically presents us with a way of achieving our own Self-realisation.

May this collection of treasures of spiritual wisdom serve as a marker, nourishment and guide for all travellers on their spiritual journey.

Harriet Bucher (Hemlata) and Renate Lavicka
(Radha), Vienna, July 1993

What is Yoga?

Yoga is a universal principle that incorporates the totality of all cosmic functions.

Yoga is union.

Union results in equilibrium and balance.

Yoga not only means peace and harmony between all human beings, but also the union of all elements and cosmic forces. The entire universe was created in this way, as our planet and all others were created through the union of different elements. In the process of creation, the unifying cosmic principle manifests itself, by whatever name you call it – God, cosmic energy, love or Yoga.

In the universe there are thousands of sun systems, whose course is directed by the one consciousness. This one, eternal, unchangeable consciousness, which is always awake, is *PARABRAHMA*. It exists in each and every atom.

PARABRAHMA is not a person. It is the supreme principle that has no form or name. We can only call it Light, Sound, the Absolute, Truth or Eternity. And this is Yoga: the consciousness that is constantly awake. In contrast to the sleeping consciousness, Yoga is creative. It is creation in action.

Human consciousness can be divided into four stages: unconscious, subconscious, conscious and super conscious. Above these four incomplete and continuously changing states of consciousness stands the all-pervasive cosmic consciousness. It is always awake and conscious of itself.

In our sleep we do not seem to perceive our surroundings. However, if we were totally unconscious, we would not remember any of our dreams after waking. But as we do often remember our dreams, a part of our consciousness is obviously still active even during our sleep. This consciousness observes everything and allows us to remember that we have dreamt or slept deeply. It is, so to speak, the "consciousness in the consciousness".

When the human consciousness becomes "enlightened", or completely awakened, a union between the individual and cosmic consciousness is formed. This, then, is the transcendental union and the spiritual realisation of which the Yogis speak. Such a Yogi is a "knowing one"; he knows past, present and future. The three aspects of time melt into each other to form an indivisible manifestation with no beginning or end. Achieving this consciousness is the aim of the *Gyana Yogis.*

In meditation, only the one who carries within himself the deep desire to know the truth is going to succeed. Those who meditate with the intention of achieving special powers will not be successful.

Countless disciples wish for a *SIDDHI* (supernatural power); if, however, they are given a mystical experience they become afraid. It is not enough just to achieve extraordinary *siddhis,* one also has to know how to deal with them. Most people find it hard enough to master their own normal level of consciousness.

Realisation means the awakening of the consciousness in the *ANAHATA CHAKRA* (heart centre). In *SAMADHI* (state of highest consciousness), it will rise to the thousand-petalled Lotus of the *SAHASRARA CHAKRA* (crown centre on the top of the head), and then return again to the boundlessness of the *Anahata Chakra.* This is the experience of the Absolute. This is Yoga. This is union.

We exist in Yoga, whether we are conscious of it or not. We are unified consciousness, and in reality, we are not separate from one other. Only through our ignorance have we lost the memory of this union and identify ourselves wrongly as separate individuals.

But it is possible to regain our consciousness of this union. We are part of the ONE and have a great longing to return to our source.

To practice Yoga in Daily Life® means to walk the path of reuniting with God.

In the *Bhagavad Gita,* Lord Krishna says to Arjuna, "I also gave this Yoga to the Sun God."

Who is this "Sun God"? The sun is not a person. The sun is a part of the cosmos. The sun allows and preserves our life through her light, her power and her radiation of energy, or whatever else you wish to call it. This force that concentrated itself to become the sun is the Yoga that Lord Krishna talked about.

Krishna also says: *"I manifest myself through my Yoga power."*

In each and every incarnation, whether divine, human or animal, the manifestation of the divine light happens exclusively through the power of Yoga. Only those who understand this understand the meaning of Yoga.

Five blind people describe an elephant:

One touches the trunk and thinks that the elephant must look like a pipe. The second feels the tail and claims that an elephant resembles a rope. The third holds the leg and describes the elephant as a column. The fourth touches the belly and declares that the elephant is like a drum. The fifth grabs the ear of the elephant and compares it with a butterfly.
Each one of them describes the elephant according to their own individual experience.

There are also various opinions within Yoga. Yoga includes different techniques and several paths. As each part of the elephant has its own name and meaning, each part of Yoga is also important and meaningful.

The Yogi who feels one with everything, with God and himself, has grasped the reality of Yoga.

A disciple asked his Master, "Master, can one experience true happiness on earth?"
The Master said, "Yes."
The disciple continued to question him, "Why then do I feel unhappy so often? How can I find true happiness?"
The master answered with a question:
"Who are you? Try first to find out who you are. If you don't even know that, how can you say whether you are happy or unhappy?"

This is the basic question that lies at the beginning of Yoga: *"Who am I?"*

I am not the body.
I am not the thoughts.
I am not the mind.

"Who are you then?"
The legs are not the elephant, the trunk is not the elephant, and the ears are not the elephant. What, then, is the elephant in reality?

We need to look for and discover the answers!

The Yogis found the answer:

> *I am SAT-CHIT-ANANDA*
> *I am Truth, Consciousness and Bliss.*

I am the reality that never changes. What changes is unreality. I am *CHITTA, CHETANYA* – the conscious witness of the changing states of consciousness.

I am not this worldly consciousness that continuously fluctuates between sleeping and waking. I am the transcendent consciousness that is ever awake and the witness of all.

I am not unhappy, not suffering, nor sick. I am bliss. My Self is the reality.
I am *SAT-CHIT-ANANDA*.

Whoever has experienced this Truth within oneself rises forever above the play of life on this earth.

Intellectual knowledge is definitely not always a sign of higher consciousness. Through studies you can gain worldly knowledge, but that does not necessarily result in the development of a higher level of consciousness. The intellect is extremely limited and only goes as far as our last breath, as after death all our intellectual knowledge means nothing.

A realised person cannot be recognised through their academic titles; they possess another kind of knowledge. Such a person reveals a pure wisdom.

This knowingness is achieved through MANANA, the discerning observation of inner and outer experiences. This leads to the recognition of:

> BRAHMA SATYA JAGATA MITHYA
> *Brahman, the universal consciousness, is reality, the world is unreality.*

At the level of consciousness in which we generally exist, we experience the world as reality. Through our senses, we see it, we feel it and we exist in it. The *Gyana Yogi,* however, is aware of the deceptive net of MAYA (worldly illusion) that keeps us imprisoned.

Recognise what is real. Rise above your animal instincts and go beyond the limitations of your intellect. Much more exists than this world that is perceived by your senses, and your present consciousness is only transitory.

> *A disciple posed this question to his master:*
> *"If I am only able to experience myself as an individual being, how can I achieve universal consciousness? How can I reunite myself?"*
> *The master responded,*

"Love unites. Where there is knowledge, there is love, and where there is ignorance, hate exists. Where there is love, there is unity. Where there is no love, duality divides."
The disciple continued to question the master:
"What is love?"
The master replied, "God is love, and love is God."

What does love mean, and what is God?
The answer can be found in the teachings of Yoga.

Over the course of their development, human beings have reached a point where they began to rise above their animal consciousness. They have learned how to pay attention to each other's needs, how to develop understanding for other beings, and as a consequence, started to think about what it means to be human.

Slowly, spiritual love developed within them. This love has four aspects.

The first aspect of this love has three parts: PRAYER, MEDITA-TION AND MANTRA – these will reunite us with God.

You cannot change the nature of a person by force – even if you wash a piece of coal a thousand times, it will not become white. There are people who do not wish to believe in God. But even these "atheists" have a chance to be one with God, because the second aspect of this love is the use of a special talent or skill for the benefit and joy of others. To compose a song and to give soul to the sounds, so that people are inspired and uplifted, is like a meditation. God lives in each sound, and the harmony in the tones is like the unification of individuals. But not everyone has such artistic talents.

The third aspect of this love is to lead people via the written or spoken word to love, harmony and knowing. The human mind has served as the medium for all the holy books of the world that have continued to inspire mankind. This task, however, is not easy. Only that which one carries within can be written or spoken. Only the pure and positive consciousness can be the medium for the divine.

> *A fly settled on a container with sandalwood paste, but it was completely oblivious to the delicious scent. When someone with muddy shoes entered the room, it immediately left the precious sandalwood paste to sit in the middle of the mud. The fly was attracted to it because it corresponded to its inherent qualities. It is the nature of a fly to live in the dirt.*

There are also people who are unable to perceive anything positive anywhere because it is completely covered and buried inside them. Everyone attracts to themselves whatever they identify with. For this reason, it is incredibly important to purify your own thoughts. People look at life with the colours that they have given it. To recognise this fact is an important step for our continued development.

Those who are unable to attain union through prayer, artistic activities or writing can try to find this love through *Karma Yoga*.

The fourth aspect of this love is love through work. "Work is worship – work is prayer". This is the essence of *Karma Yoga*. Rabindranath Tagore, the famous poet and philosopher, said,

> *"When I sing, God loves me; when I work, He respects me."*

8

Karma is created through thoughts, words and actions. For this reason, these three activities should always be directed positively. Work should not be done just to make money; it also needs to be useful to others. Don't create weapons; instead create flowers. Why? Because flowers evoke love, while weapons evoke hatred.

These different aspects of love correspond with the different talents and inclinations in people. Each one of us has our own individual way of accessing God. Accordingly, in Yoga we differentiate between four main paths:

BHAKTI YOGA	the path of love and devotion to God,
RAJA YOGA	the path of practice, experience and meditation,
GYANA YOGA	the path of study and philosophy
KARMA YOGA	the path of selfless service and helping

However, the essence of all paths which lead to liberation is: TO LOVE, TO HELP, TO PROTECT, TO UNDERSTAND, TO FORGIVE and TO GIVE. No killing or stealing. All religions of this world whose teachings are based on these principles spring from Yoga and lead into Yoga.

Yoga is the path to God, the path to the Self, to peace, harmony and enlightenment.

Four pillars – *DHARMA, ARTHA, KAMA* and *MOKSHA* – form the supports of the house of each human life. And only if these pillars are strongly and firmly built can they support the house.

DHARMA means task, responsibility and duty towards our society, family and the environment.
ARTHA means wealth/prosperity, both material and spiritual.

KAMA here means activity and creativity.
MOKSHA is liberation.
DHARMA, ARTHA and *KAMA* together lead to *MOKSHA*.

An important condition for the completion of your life's purpose is good health – physical, mental, social and spiritual health. Health means the harmonious balance of all aspects of our life.

The system of Indian medicine, *AYURVEDA,* uses primarily natural resources such as roots, flowers, leaves, fruits and minerals for healing. These lead the person to health naturally by restoring the right balance in body and mind. *AYUR* means life and *VEDA* means knowledge – *AYURVEDA* is "knowledge about life".

Healthy nutrition forms the external support for good health. Physical practices compliment the state of health by supporting from within.

The first step in Yoga are the physical practices, or the *ASANAS*. There are 8.4 million *asanas*, of which 84 are referred as the major *asanas*. The movements and positions of the *asanas* imitate the sequential flow of movements presented within nature and regenerate the life force of the nervous system and physical body through their psychosomatic effects.

Apart from good nutrition and the practice of *asanas,* regular practice of *PRANAYAMA, CONCENTRATION* and *MEDITATION* are essential.

For the development of a mature human personality a comprehensive education is of great significance. An education that includes body, psyche and consciousness enables a continuous, harmonious development towards the goal of God-realisation.

Yoga is both a philosophy and a path to realisation. Yoga leads us to the reality of the highest consciousness. But that one who does not know how to drink returns thirsty from the spring. The great saint and gifted poet Kabirdas said,

"I had to laugh, when I saw the fish thirsty in the water."

Only through our own practice and experience is it possible to really understand what Yoga means. Only in this way can you develop *PARAVIDYA,* the knowledge of God, which is in harmony with reality. People are prepared to do a lot for this body, which is only transitory and will leave them soon, but very little for their spiritual development, which is eternal.

If you have put your trust in me, listen to what I tell you. Do not waste your life. Use the time that is given to you as a human: believe in God, pray to God and feel God. God comes to you in the form that you carry in your heart. Purify your thoughts and do not waste your time, otherwise you will be very sorry one day.

Practise Yoga in Daily Life® — it will lead you to your goal. I wish you a pure consciousness, God's blessing and divine guidance.

The Four Pathways in Yoga

KARMA YOGA

The highest principle of *Karma* Yoga is SEVA (service). NISHKAM KARMA – selfless action – is the best type of *karma*. God incarnated on this planet to serve mankind selflessly, without expecting anything in return. If your actions are based on any expectations, ego or pride, then it is not really true service.

NISHKAM KARMA leads to liberation. But SAKAM KARMA, selfish action, only creates new desires that bind us.

Always act and serve with love. Serving and giving are part of our most important tasks in life.

RAJA YOGA

AHIMSA is the highest principle of *Raja Yoga.* It means not to hurt or kill anyone, neither human beings nor animals. Without *ahimsa* there is no selfless service. Serving means love. Love means *Ahimsa.* SEVA and AHIMSA belong together.

If you love someone you will not hurt or kill them. If you feel love inside you, you will not think or speak negatively.

Raja Yoga teaches that the principle of AHIMSA is the highest principle of the *Yamas* and *Niyamas,* the inner and outer disciplines.

GYANA YOGA

The highest principle of *Gyana Yoga* is ATMA GYANA. *Atma gyana* means Self-realisation and self-recognition. Achieving liberation is impossible unless you truly know yourself. However, this knowledge can only develop when *ahimsa,* love, and GURU KRIPA, the grace of the Master, are present.

> MOKSHA MULAM GURU KRIPA
> The root of liberation is *Guru kripa.*

Gyana Yoga tells us to "live in this world with VIVEKA."

VIVEKA means discernment. Discriminate between what is good and bad, and be detached. Attachment takes you away from your goal and leads towards additional and new addictions. Attachments to people, possessions or money are the cause of many of our problems and much of our suffering. Attachment is caused by ignorance. It an iron chain binding you. You cannot move freely anymore. Attachment leads to suffering, pain and destruction. It prevents you from meditation, relaxation, concentration and prayer.

That is why two important principles are emphasized in *Gyana Yoga*: VAIRAGYA (non-attachment) and VIVEKA (discrimination).

> *Where there is VIVEKA there is AHIMSA*
> *Where there is AHIMSA there is SEVA.*
> *Where there is SEVA there is AHIMSA.*
> *Where there is AHIMSA there is VIVEKA.*

BHAKTI YOGA

The highest principle of *bhakti* is GURU BHAKTI, devotion and love for the *Guru*.

To love your parents and siblings is easy, as you have parents in each life. Even animals have a mother and a father. GURU BHAKTI is rare, and only human beings can develop it. GURU BHAKTI requires total surrender. That means to always be ready.

Mahaprabhuji said in a *bhajan*:

GURU BHAKTA JAGATA ME NAR HE.
The *Guru bhaktas* are the real people in this world.

Those who have no GURU BHAKTI, no love, are like animals. Eating, sleeping and procreating, animals can also do. If you have no *Bhakti,* no love of God, then what is the meaning of your life?

The greatest mistakes a human can make are not to recognise the value of this life, and not to strive for Self-realisation. Whoever dies without reaching Self-realisation does not know what is going to happen to him.

Think about the meaning of your life. Think why are you here? What is your purpose?

Try to understand the meaning and the purpose of your life. The opportunity to be born as a human is rare. You should not miss this opportunity by wasting this lifetime.

Realise the highest principles of KARMA, RAJA, GYANA and BHAKTI YOGA in your life.

GURU BHAKTA JAGATA ME NAR HE
FIR UNKO KISKA DARA HE

GURU BHAKTA THE ROHITA TARA
HARICANDRA RAJA ADHIKARA
JYARA HOGAYA NAMA AMARA HE

GURU SEVA ME MORADHAJA RAJA
TYAG DIVI SABA JAGA KI LAJA
MANADHARI KI SABRA JABARA HE

DHRUVA BALAKA GURU AGYADHARAI
UNAKI DHAMA ACALA KARA DARI
JINE KIYA KALA KO SARA HE

GURU BHAKTA THE JANAKA VIDEHI
SRI KRISNA OR RAMAVANDRAJI
VO BAN GAYA APA ISVARA HE

BRAHMA VISNU MAHESVARA DEVA
SAB KERE SATAGURUJI KI SEVA
SAB HI SATAGURU KA CAKAR HE

SVAMI DIPA SATYA SAMAJHAVE
GURU BHAKTI BINA JIVA DUKHA PAVE
GURU KARA DE BHALI NAJARA HE

A person who has found his Guru no longer needs to be afraid.

Rohita, Tara and Harichandra were devoted to their Guru,
And their names became immortal.

15

King Moradhaja renounced this world,
He devoted himself totally to meditation and to the
service of his Guru.

Dhruva obeyed the directions of his Guru even as a child,
And reached immortality through unswerving worship.

King Janaka, Sri Krishna and Ramachandra
Were devotees of their Guru and became divine
themselves.

Brahma, Vishnu and Maheshwara
Are all servants of the Satguru.
Mahaprabhuji puts his humble request to you:
Please look at us with your grace!!

Bhagwan Sri Deep Narayan Mahaprabhuji

Who am I?

Problems only exist for as long as we have no clarity about who we truly are. For example, we say, "I am Franz. I am a man. I am Austrian. I am a clerk. I am a father." We identify ourselves with our name, gender, nationality, profession – with different things, depending upon what seems to be most important to us.

The unexpressed basis for these ideas is our identification with the body. The body, however, is only transitory. It is for this reason that, for some people, life appears to be like a candle flame; once it has been blown out it no longer exists. However, the concept that we appear out of nothing at birth and cease to exist when we die seems unconvincing and unbelievable. On the other hand, existence without the body is hard to imagine.

All these ideas based on our identification with the body, and all the different theories about life and death, only demonstrate how ignorant we are. What then are we to believe? Which path leads us to the realisation of our true Self?

We resemble tourists standing at a crossroad, not knowing which road to take. When we find ourselves at such a crossroad trying to figure out which path is the right one, we try to look ahead to see where the different paths lead. But for us to do this, our physical sense organ is not sufficient, and we need to use our "inner eye".

And perhaps we don't need to go anywhere. Perhaps it is only our ignorance that makes us believe that we have to follow some path.

Where is the centre of the universe?

The centre of the universe is, for everyone, exactly where they are right now. Reality is there where all paths end. And we can only reach this through our efforts and practice. *Kriya*, *mantra*, prayer and meditation are our supports on this path.

Choose the path that leads you to yourself – the path to your Self.

When you start the journey to your Self, your viewpoint changes completely. At first you see many paths leading away from the crossroads. Then suddenly you realise that these paths don't lead away from where you are. To the contrary, they all lead *to* where you are.

You yourself are the centre and the goal. Each path leads to you; you don't need to go anywhere.

It all depends on the way you look at it. When you pray: "Lead me to thee, oh Lord!" you want to go to God. If, however, you call Him, "Come to me, oh Lord!" you are asking for Him to be present with you. God can come to you faster than you can go to Him. He is already here, within you.

And where is that?

When you touch your body, you say, "this is *my* head, *my* arm, *my* hair" etc. But who are *you*, when you regard these body parts as merely belonging to you? In this way you make it clear that you *have* a body, but that you *are not* the body.

You also speak of *your* feelings and *your* thoughts – but what are you really? The body will die. The truth, however, is eternal. Feelings and thoughts change, but the truth always stays the same.

What are you? What is reality?

You cannot find your Self within your body. People used to be of the opinion that the soul resided in the heart. If you transplant a heart, do you also transplant the soul? Obviously, that is not the case. The *ATMA,* the soul, cannot be removed. The soul is like space. You can remove something from a space, just as you can from a room. However, the space itself cannot be removed. You can carry something from one space to another, but you cannot transport the space itself. The *Atma* is not fixed to a specific part of the body.

Another viewpoint is that the *Atma* is evenly distributed throughout the whole body. If that was the case you would miss a piece of your soul if a particular part of your body was amputated.

When a living being dies, the life force does not immediately leave the body, still life force is present in some cells of the body. This is how people came to realise that it is only the consciousness that leaves the body.

You are pure consciousness!

However, by forming the hypothesis that you are the consciousness, you are again creating duality. I am "here", and "there" is the consciousness that I am talking about.

The question cannot be answered this way. You yourself have to experience what you are. It is like someone trying to explain to you the taste of a food that is foreign to you. It cannot be explained to you, you will have to taste it yourself.

The Yogi who practices daily and repeats his MANTRA comes to realise the truth.

The physical form does not limit the *Atma*. *Atma* radiates far beyond it. Is this radiation (the Aura as it is generally known) the light of the soul, or the soul itself?

You may not feel satisfied with these answers. You will need to find the answers yourself through your own experience and through your own practice under the guidance of a Master who knows the true answers.

A shepherd once found a little lion cub that had been abandoned. He took it home with him and raised it along with his sheep.

One day a big lion came close to the herd. All the sheep ran away in terror and so did the little lion cub that thought it was a sheep.

Seeing this, the great lion was wondering, "How come this young lion is afraid of me and runs away with the sheep? I will catch him and find out."

The old lion caught the young lion that was trembling in terror, and asked him, "Why are you trembling? You are not a sheep, but a lion like me!"

"Oh, no! I know who I am! I was born here and I am a sheep like all the other sheep here," the young lion answered in despair.

When the older lion saw that his explanations were fruit-less and the cub did not want to believe him, he said, "Come with me, I will show you who you really are. You will see for yourself. Then you will believe me."

He guided the young lion to the water and told him, "Look at your image in the water and then tell me, who do you resemble, the sheep – or me, the lion?"

Then the lion cub saw its real identity. It lost its fear and moved on, joining the old lion.

We are like the lion cub – full of fear and ignorance. *Gurudeva* is like the older lion that comes to us so that we can experience our true Self and experience that we are the *Atma*, the Divine Self.

Don't be afraid. Don't run away. Look into your inner mirror and you will recognise who you really are. Move into your inner self and recognise your Self in your meditation.

You don't need to go anywhere, because all paths lead to you!

Realise SANATANA DHARMA.

SANATANA means relationship. Most people understand relationship primarily as the relationship to your blood family. But *sanatan* relates to all living beings – the true relationship in *Atma*. All living beings are God's creatures – humans as well as animals and plants.

One creator created all life. That ONE lives in all, and all live in that ONE. If you fill 20 cups with water and place them outside so that the moon is reflected in all of them, you will see the same moon in each cup, regardless of the colour, shape or size of the cups. And in the same way God is reflected in all, no matter what kind of living being it is. For this reason, the true relationship is our *sanatana*, our relationship, with God.

We are all a part of God.

And this is not about quantity, but quality. Only things of the same quality can unite; fire with fire, water with water, and air with air.

DHARMA means duty, religion or principle. The *dharma* of humans is to protect life, to understand others, to love, to forgive and to give. Those people who are not conscious of their *dharma* develop pride, ego, greed, jealousy and hatred. Why? Because they have strayed away from the right path. Those who do not recognise their *dharma* cannot reach their goal.

With Self-realisation the *Mantra* SO HAM appears.

SO HAM means *"That I am – I am That".*

AHAM BRAHMASMI – *I am the ATMA who is BRAHMA.*

For as long as there is no realisation of this, no liberation or union can happen.

When the tiny little existence of your Self unites with God, all individuality ends. Knowledge, knower and object become one – this is what we call *SAMADHI*.

KNOWLEDGE means that you know who you are, that you are the KNOWER. What do you want to know? You want to recognise your Self. Your Self is the OBJECT.

WHO AM I? With this realisation the *DHARMA* of human life is attained.

Our Phenomenon

The whole universe is an illusion, a "phenomenon". This phenomenon is limitless; there are countless functions, systems, elements and principles, which are part of it.

Inside this 'Macro' Cosmos the individual exists like a 'Micro' Cosmos. The cosmic phenomenon is called *Brahmanda*, while the individual phenomenon is *Pinda.*

From our limited viewpoint, even our individual phenomenon seems to be infinite because in reality we know very little about ourselves. Most people know no more about themselves other than what they see reflected in the mirror, or the characteristics by which others judge them. They are not aware of the deeper connections to their physiological and psychological functions. Who of us knows from which "organ" emotion comes, or which point in us is touched when we hear something joyful or sad? We think that the source of our feelings is the heart or the brain, but this assumption is not the truth.

Most of our problems do not come from the present, but from times long gone by. Even though we know that the past has no reality, often it is not possible for us to let go of the impressions from our past.

One woman who came to me for a consultation told me that she had been in a concentration camp during the war. She had seen horrific things and had terrible experiences that she could never forget. Even though it was clear to her that this time was well and truly gone, she was still tortured with the fear and the hate that she had felt then. She wanted to know from me how she could forget these experiences.

I said to her, "Some things we can't forget, we can only forgive."

Where is the seat of our memories, or our qualities such as joy, sadness, hate, fear, jealousy and love? If they were all stored in our brain, it would not be possible for us to have memories of past lives, because when leaving the physical body all our memories and qualities would be lost each time. Is our phenomenon really that limited?

How is it possible that the place of the *Atma* could be in the brain or the heart, when we often feel ourselves thousands of kilometres away from it?

Yoga shows us the way to understand the mystery of the individual and the cosmic phenomenon. Knowledge can resolve everything. But we do not mean intellectual knowledge, but rather *Atma gyana,* true knowledge of the *Atma.*

The reality is the *Atma.* It is not the body, the mind or consciousness, nor the thoughts or feelings, but our true Self. Generally, we do not know much about this Self of ours, only the name; just as, for example, we may know a relative who lives overseas by name, or via letter, but we have never seen them personally. We have no real idea of what this relative is truly like.

Similarly, we only know the word *Atma* – soul, Self or whatever we call the Divine within us. We speak to it, we feel it, but we have never seen it face to face.

Atma gyana leads to recognition and realisation of the Self. As long as this realisation has not occurred, we will always have problems in this world as well as in the astral plane – not only in this life, but also in the next one. A lot of people believe that after death their problems are over. This is a big mistake because everyone has to return to Earth to work off their *karmas.*

Not only does our individual phenomenon contain our personal Self, but it is our own universe in which we live. Our phenomenon possesses many qualities and divisions. These are called *koshas* (sheaths).

You can visualise the *koshas* in the following way:

> *Imagine an empty block of land on which a house is being erected. Walls are being erected in the house so there will be rooms. The rooms will be furnished with the tattvas (elements). The function of the prana is to bring together and connect the elements with each other. Prana fills the rooms, but uses no space itself. And the Atma, our true Self, exists within these partitions and rooms.*

Liberation, or *moksha,* means the liberation of the *Atma* from the five *Koshas.* As long as the *koshas* are not dissolved, you cannot become one with the Universe. You are a single drop and the universe is the ocean. When you use this comparison, your individual phenomenon is completely invisible, that's how tiny it is. Only when it has been cleared and totally purified of all attachments, can the drop of the small, limited "I" again become one with the ocean of the infinite Divine consciousness. Once the drop has become one with the ocean, it no longer exists as a single drop. This is how to understand *moksha.* It is possible for this drop – the individual – to release itself once again from the ocean of Divine consciousness. In doing so, the individual is "reborn". However, it is not reborn in exactly the same form and composition as before because other components of the ocean will now be a part of it.

A Yogi does not judge heaven to be superior to hell. To him both planes are still limited, because where the sky ends, hell starts and vice versa. God, however, is unlimited. To look at heaven as a reward and hell as a punishment only serves to maintain the ethical and social rules on earth. Heaven and hell only exist in this world, and both are created by us.

God is invisible, omnipresent and complete. He exists in the good and in the bad.

Mantra and meditation are your supports and guides as you explore your phenomenon, and through these you attain *Atma gyana*. With *Atma gyana* you can transcend the *koshas* and finally unite with God.

Our Mind

Our mind sometimes resembles a wild elephant or a tiger; sometimes it becomes a beggar and other times a king. Sometimes it is sad, and then again it can be joyous. It is always restless and discontent. We try in many ways to satisfy the mind, but usually never succeed for long.

The great Saint Kabirdas said,

> *"As long as you cannot control your mind, you will not be able to overcome attachment and suffering. As long as you are unable to kill your mind, you will not be able to kill your problems."*

There are two functions of our psyche which are outside our conscious control: ASA and TRISHNA.

- *Asa* means expectation, longing.
- *Trishna* is the "thirst", the desire that makes us suffer with the longing.

Kabirdas said, *"As long as you have not overcome those two, you cannot overcome the mind."*

Trishna is like a Fata Morgana[1]; you think something is there, whereas in reality there is nothing.

---

[1] Fata Morgana was a fairy enchantress skilled in the art of changing shape. It is also a relatively rare complex mirage that occurs occasionally in Alaska.

The mind is thirsty, restless, discontent; it is forever searching and constantly changing. It is because of the mind that many people get confused.

When you can control your mind, you have become the master. Then you can achieve anything.

It takes discipline and VIVEKA (discrimination) to steer the mind. To be able to achieve this you need to be able to watch and master your senses. This is not easy; the mind and the senses can make people blind and egotistical.

Only through practice and GURU KRIPA – the blessing of the Guru – can you learn to control the mind.

In his bhajan, BHAJO RE MANVA SRI PRABHU DIP DAYAL, Holy Guruji said,

> "Oh mind, meditate always on the blessed Mahaprabhuji."
> He is Parabrahma, the creator of the universe.
> One look from Mahaprabhuji can liberate you."

When Mahaprabhuji looked someone in the eyes, they were filled with light through and through. Mahaprabhuji manifested on this earth to protect all souls. He is PARI-PURANA: totally perfect in every way. Whoever meditates on Mahaprabhuji with their whole heart will be liberated from maya and freed from death and rebirth. This liberation can happen instantly and in this world, not only after death.

Mahaprabhuji is the Supreme. The blessed ones who lived on earth in His lifetime were able to see Him in His human form. Even today many bhaktas can see Him, because He appears in pure hearts. Wherever there are doubts and complexes

God cannot appear. Anyone who has the opportunity to see the blessed Master in person is the happiest of people.

The light of Mahaprabhuji shines in the hearts of those who have *mantra*. Live in purity and devotion, without doubts and insecurities. It takes a long time to purify the mind.

Prana

Every atom contains *prana*, or life energy. *Prana* is different to oxygen, electricity and vitality – these are qualities of *prana*, but not the whole. *Prana* and oxygen surround our planet. Water also contains *prana*, but humans are unable to exist in this form of *prana*.

Prana is beyond the elements. Elements require space. *Prana* needs no space. When we fill a hollow area with water, it will only hold as much water as that particular space can contain. Even air occupies space. *Prana* does not. *Prana* is like light. You can light as many lamps in one room as you wish – the room will become lighter, but the light does not take any space.

Prana is distributed throughout the whole cosmos. It always looks for an object where it can gather. It even begins to flow into the smallest atom. Our *Atma* is *prana* and *prana* is God.

The *Atma* itself is a huge concentration of *prana*. Besides the actual *Atma* that exists within us, the "*Master Atma*" as we could call it, millions of different small souls or *pranas* are living in our body. Just as in a beehive, thousands of bees will gather around a queen, but when the queen leaves the hive the other bees will also disperse. In the same manner the body of a living being will slowly disintegrate after death.

When God manifests in a physical body, a huge amount of *prana* collects within the cosmos and incarnates. This person possesses all abilities commensurate with the highest state of perfection. They are God incarnate.

Each word spoken by such an *avatara* is the pure, unadulterated truth. Their presence has an immensely strong radiation of *prana* in this world, because *prana* will radiate through each of their movements. Each word and each of their thoughts contain a huge amount of *prana*.

The *Atma* that lives in a body travels through an enormously long developmental process during which it is subjected to the cycles and laws of nature.

I remember this saying about autumn:

Leaves are falling off the tree – the wind blows them away.
Who knows where they are falling?
Who knows if they ever come back together again?

This same process also happens at birth; the umbilical cord that connects mother and child is cut, and the fate of the child takes its own independent course.

Each leaf changes its form as it withers. In the same way, we cannot assume we will come back to earth in the same form.

Our master soul, the *Atma*, wanders through the different planes of the Universe in accordance with the cosmic law. The other constituent parts of *prana* form into new shapes according to the natural law, becoming plants, animals or people. The natural law is part of the cosmic law. Our path is determined according to the meandering of our destiny; however, we all have the same goal of achieving union with God.

Recognise the golden opportunity in being born as a human. Work on yourself and purify your consciousness. God consciousness lies hidden in the human consciousness. In God consciousness, not even the smallest element of a negative quality exists. Such qualities indicate a lower level of consciousness as exists in the animal kingdom. As humans we need to rise above this level.

Develop love, compassion and all the other positive, divine qualities within yourself. Yoga offers the best method of support to purify and overcome all negative qualities.

Everyone participates in *karma* in three ways: as the doer, as the receiver, and as either the beneficiary or the victim. Take care to transfer your energy into useful work and into doing good, as all your actions will ultimately reflect back on you.

All your relationships and connections in this world will end with death. Because of this, search for the one connection that is timeless and limitless. And use all your knowledge, your drive and your strength to realise the eternal bond. Only this will make you happy and content.

The Koshas

ANNAMAYA KOSHA

Annamaya Kosha means the "body of nourishment". The physical body forms itself from this *kosha*. The physical body is not everything, but it would be a mistake to discard it as unimportant. It is very important to us, because only through the body can we work and have an influence on things. With the body we create good and bad deeds, or *karmas*. Without the body we cannot do anything.

Our physical and psychological functions are affected by our nourishment, environment, education and society. Food does not only sustain the physical body, but through our food we also absorb energy, which nourishes our outer layers – the astral, mental, intellectual and causal bodies. Each of these bodies needs its own specific nourishment.

For example, in conversation a type of nourishment takes place through which certain needs of the emotional and causal bodies are being satisfied. Occasionally, we simply need someone to talk to. After that we feel relieved, free and relaxed.

Each word that we absorb affects us not only in a spiritual and psychological sense, but also in a physical sense. Words affect us a thousand times more than we suspect. A single word can either elevate or destroy us.

Humans have also developed their intellect through the ability of speech. This development resulted in an increase in consciousness. And in this way, by learning to discern between good and bad, joy and pain, humans slowly developed an understanding of the purpose and meaning of human existence.

Again and again saints incarnate on earth to enlighten us about our own true, divine nature. They come to teach us how to recognise the divine nature within us, and what we should or should not do. They also teach us about the effects of nutrition and recommend that we follow a *sattvic* diet, which balances and strengthens the body. God gave us this body equipped with all the functions necessary to take everything it needs for its existence from very small amounts of food.

Prajapati, the Creator, truly is the best architect. He created a perfect human being. Why, then, do we have to suffer so much? The sufferings of humans began when they lost their trust in God and relied only on their own limited experiences and their intellect.

There are two worlds: one is created by God, the other by humans. The world that is created by humans is very imperfect, whereas the world created by God is totally perfect. Due to our blindness we are not capable of recognising the perfection of God's world, and some even refuse to recognise it.

A scientist, full of vain intellectual pride, thought he knew all about life. According to him, creation was less than complete, and so he felt it was up to humans to improve upon it. He thought people who believed in God were foolish and backward. To him, research and science were the only values in life through which a human being could achieve anything.

One day he encountered a Yogi, sitting under a cherry tree, meditating.

He asked the Yogi, "What are you doing?"

"I am meditating," said the Yogi.

"What does that mean – meditating?"

"To think of God and be with God."

"Who is God?"

"God is the creator of all."

"Oh, if that is so, this God is not very clever!"

"Why do you believe that?" the Yogi asked, surprised.

The scientist answered, "For example, take this cherry tree under which you are sitting. It is about ten metres high, and even though it is so big and strong it carries only tiny little fruit. And look over there in the field where huge melons are growing on small tender stalks. It would be more appropriate to have big fruit growing on big plants and small ones on small plants."

The Yogi thought, "Please God give me a sign, so that I can open the eyes of this man."

At that moment a cherry fell off a branch and landed on the head of the scientist. He wiped it off with his hand and did not take any further notice.

But the Yogi asked the man, "What just happened?"

"Nothing in particular, it was just a small cherry that fell on my head."

"Don't say it was nothing in particular! Think what would have happened if God, according to your logic, had grown big melons on this tree and small cherries in the field? Then you would have had a melon weighing several kilos falling on your head and you would certainly have been injured!"

"Oh," said the man, "that's an interesting thought. I will have to think about it."

The Yogi answered him, "Meditate on it and soon you will understand more."

The scientist said goodbye to the Yogi and returned to his home. Angrily he thought, "Why did that cherry have to fall on my head, and why did this Yogi give me an argument that I could not contradict?"

The words of the Yogi did not leave him, and he actually started to meditate. And soon a peace entered into his heart that he had never experienced before. He continued to meditate and when another month had passed he noticed that he had started to understand the world and human beings much better. His heart opened more and more.

One day he had a marvellous vision: the Yogi appeared to him, and his body dissolved in light. Out of this light a wonderful divine manifestation formed. God smiled at him and spoke, "It was me whom you met as the Yogi under the cherry tree. For your sake I went there to finally lead you onto the right path."

After this meditation the man went back to the same cherry tree. Again, the Yogi was sitting there in meditation. The scientist greeted him, sat next to him and began to meditate. After some time when he opened his eyes, he was alone; the Yogi had disappeared.

From now on he continued his meditation under this tree where he had encountered his Guru for the first time. Next to it, he built an ashram, where he now lives. An eternal flame was lit on the altar in honour of God.

In hindsight, we can often recognise a seemingly meaningless, accidental event as a mystery of divine grace and mercy. A single moment or a single word can change our whole life.

Annamaya kosha represents our bio-energetic field. This field has a radiation of several hundred metres beyond the physical body. With each physical movement we release energy.

When we lead a pure *sattvic* life, our radiation is a flawless, clear light of harmony, health and love.

Physical and mental strength come only through discipline. Through discipline we store our energy rather than destroying it. To exercise discipline with our food is a very important form of self-control, because,

"We do not live to eat, but we eat to live!"

Millions of people suffer from hunger due to political reasons. In countries growing the most splendid fruits, people are starving because the whole harvest is being exported to industrialised nations. We use precious woods to make furniture and paper and destroy more and more irreplaceable forests. Dominated by the greed of our senses, we destroy our environment and kill innocent creatures. Countless animals suffer torture in the name of "scientific" research, and millions of animals have to die daily because we find their flesh "tasty."

I recall one of my talks where an elderly woman fixed her gaze on me intensely. Her exploring look was so obvious that this woman stayed in my memory, even though there were hundreds of other listeners in the room.

The next day one of my disciples told me, that her grandmother – the woman who had stared at me so intently – had been very concerned, because according to her I would not live very much longer. When my disciple asked how she had come to this conclusion, she answered, "Because he does not eat any meat." Apparently, she only came to the talk to see for herself what a vegetarian would look like. Afterwards she had said, "I cannot believe that Swamiji does not eat any meat, he looks so healthy!"

I am very healthy and can only recommend that everyone lives as a vegetarian if they wish to stay completely healthy.

Our body, like a machine, needs expert treatment to function well. But it is neither necessary nor advisable to always take extra hormones or vitamins, because then the body will stop producing what it needs naturally. God equipped our body so marvellously that it is able regulate all its needs by itself, as long as we flow with nature.

To start the motor of a car, firstly we need the energy of a battery. Once the motor is running, the alternator starts working and recharges the battery. Similarly, this is how the *asanas* influence the body. They support the physical functions of the body. The practices of Yoga in Daily Life® are specifically structured to keep the body healthy. *Asanas* are the best tool to keep our bio-energetic field stable.

We are aware of our memories, feelings, diseases and other processes within our body. Yet we do not know how they came about, how they are interconnected and how they affect each other. We also know very little about the most suitable nourishment for us. Countless varieties of opinions on healthy nourishment exist today. It is most sensible to avoid extremes, to eat fresh and whole foods, and to definitely avoid eating meat.

Most of my disciples only became vegetarian after they came to me. By becoming vegetarian they all gained a deeper relationship to their own life, and more respect for the right of all other beings to live.

Unfortunately, in our society there is often still a lack of understanding about nourishment without meat.

A doctor once expressed a very negative opinion about vegetarian nutrition in an article in a magazine. For example, one of the things he wrote was that vegetarians couldn't have children. We replied to the doctor with a simple response: "Then how come India is so overpopulated?"

But such illogical and incorrect arguments are still believed by those people who do not think about what they hear or read.

Not so long ago the WHO (World Health Organization) published statistics which documented that people who are vegetarians are sick less often than those who consume meat. Diseases such as heart attacks and cancer occur less frequently in vegetarians. Additionally, many allergies are caused by eating meat.

From a health viewpoint, the consumption of meat is definitely not recommended, and from the viewpoint of spiritual ethics and protection of the environment it is definitely not recommended either. All people should ultimately decide to become vegetarians!

It is incorrect to think that we draw our energy only from the food we eat. Our willpower also makes us strong. The strength of our body is limited. The strength of our mind is limitless. This force is called *Atma Bal* in Sanskrit, meaning inner power, inner will, and is a principle of enormous energy.

Do not worry too much about your body, especially thoughts such as, *"How many vitamins should I take? I do not have enough energy. Hopefully I will not get sick."* Such thoughts create an imbalance in the function of the organs and glands; particularly those subtle functions that regulate themselves without our conscious influence. If you "think" yourself exhausted, tired and sick, then you will also feel that way. However, if you drop those thoughts, the symptoms will disappear.

I know a couple who desperately wanted a child. They had medical treatments, tried hormone therapy, acupuncture, homeopathy and much more. Nothing helped. When they had finally abandoned hope and stopped thinking about their shortcomings, the woman suddenly fell pregnant.

The physical phenomenon is endless. We know very little about our body, and often we have no understanding of why we get certain diseases or know how to treat them. If we don't even know the laws of our own body, then how can we understand the cosmic laws?

You have given me your trust and now it is my duty and responsibility to lead you to the light. For this you must keep to certain disciplines and rules. Since you have chosen to follow the spiritual path, you need to follow these disciplines and rules one hundred percent.

Sattvic nourishment, *asanas* and *pranayama* keep our bodies healthy; *mantra* and meditation will lead us to the light.

PRANAMAYA KOSHA

PRANA IS vitality, life force.

Prana enters our body with oxygen and food. *Prana* has no physical expansion; even when the room is totally filled with *prana*, it still seems empty.

Prana is also called *Ishvara Shakti*.
- *Ishvara* is the unmanifested, omnipresent God.
- *Shakti* means power, energy.

Ishvara is a part of our phenomenon. It is written in the Vedas that *Ishvara Shakti* influences us, mainly via the sun.

What does this mean? The sun represents the worldly principle. Without it there is no light, no growth and no life. For example, imagine you are very thirsty. What would be the most important thing to you now? Not food, nor sleep nor money, but water. When you are nearly dying of thirst, water represents the lifesaving principle for you. Because you do not have enough power to preserve your own life, you will need an outside power that can help you. This outside power represents the power of God. In this situation, the water principle represents God for you.

For this reason, in Indian mythology people worship the God of rain, the God of fire, the God of air and many more. God does not mean a specific person or form, but a principle – our life principle.

What then is our *Atma*? What are we? Our *Atma* is part of this life principle.

When we practice *Gyana Yoga* we gain a deeper understanding of these subtle, visible and invisible elemental powers, and become more conscious of them.

Gyana Yoga is often regarded as the highest Yoga path. *Gyana* means knowledge. This knowledge cannot be gained from one day to the next.

Often my disciples will come to me and ask how long it will take for them to reach enlightenment. They say, "Please Swamiji, give me at least an indication of how long it will take", or they say, "Swamiji, please give me enlightenment."

But enlightenment is not a piece of bread or a pill that you can simply give to someone. It is nothing material. It just appears; it comes, it is here. It depends on the inner development and purity.

It says in the Bible, "You shall not have any other Gods beside me." Most people misunderstand this saying. They think that they cannot believe in any other God besides Jesus; that Jesus is the only path to the Light. But this would mean that before the time of Jesus all people had lived in darkness and no one had been enlightened. But the Light did not come to mankind only when Jesus was born.

When Moses condemned the dancing around the golden calf, he wanted to make it clear to people that they should not worship the gold. By throwing themselves down in front of the golden image they were making the gold their God.

Often the original meaning of words changes in the course of time, and then the original understanding also gets lost. Reality can only be experienced in meditation. Whoever practices Yoga and meditates regularly will also understand the words of Jesus much better. Many people have again found their connection to the Christian teachings through their practice of Yoga in Daily Life®.

The omnipresent God is the principle of life that lives in all living beings and cares for them all. "Who has created your beak will also take care of your food." In reality, God Himself gives to each living creature the nourishment that is needed. Millions of living beings exist on this planet, and from the smallest insect to the human being they all receive their nourishment. And who cares for them? He, who gave them life. Unfortunately, humans have forgotten about this basic truth and have lost their feeling for God.

Ishvara is the life force that exists in our sun system. *Parameshvara* means the infinite, eternal, unlimited and omnipresent principle that exists throughout the whole universe. It is this power that exists in the billions of galaxies and sun systems, which all follow their own different principles.

Ishvara Shakti, or *prana*, comes to us in the light of the sun. It is written in the Vedas that in reality the sun is completely dark. *Ishvara Shakti* enlightens the sun, and this light is reflected onto us.

The light of the sun contains our life force, which is passed on in the photons. The light particles charged with this life force enter into our planetary system. They enter the atmosphere and are then attracted by an object. The moment the particle comes in contact with the object it falls apart. The energy moves into the object as *prana*; the material stays on the surface in the form of a very fine dust. The same thing happens when *prana* touches plants, animals or people.

In lifeless objects, the pure and neutral quality of the cosmic *prana* stays the same; but living beings transform the *prana* according to their own qualities, feelings and characteristics. *Prana* is altered and becomes impure. The qualities of plants are purer than the qualities of animals and humans. For this reason, plants contain so much more cosmic light, energy and life force.

When an animal is being killed 95% of its *pranic* energy is lost. Through cooking, the meat even loses the last 5%. Fresh vegetables contain 100% *pranic* energy. Through cooking we also lose nearly 80% of it. For this reason, we need to eat lots of salads and fruits, because they contain most of the pure *prana*. Many diseases can be healed through a raw food diet that cleanses and regenerates the whole body.

Pranamaya Kosha and *Annamaya Kosha* are strongly connected to one another, because both are greatly influenced by our nourishment.

Colours also have a strong effect on both these *koshas*. For example, orange draws a lot of energy from the cosmos. It works like a flame. Just as a light attracts moths, the colour orange attracts cosmic energy.

All plants grow towards the light; light means life, and life means light. Orange light purifies and attracts life force. It protects us so that negative energies cannot penetrate.

Asanas, *pranayama*, nourishment, light, air, colours and the company we keep are of paramount importance for *Annamaya Kosha* and *Pranamaya Kosha*.

MANOMAYA KOSHA

MANAS is the mind, and the power of the mind influences both the body and its surrounding environment.

How does the mind relate to our individual phenomenon? The mind has a mighty function. Yogis often compare the mind with a wild elephant, or tiger, a cobra or the devil.

The mind can destroy a person within seconds.

How is it possible to control the mind? This is no easy task. There is nothing that can bring the mind to a point of stillness, because it is as restless as the waves of the ocean in a storm.

There are five levels of consciousness: unconscious, subconscious, conscious, super consciousness and cosmic consciousness. Whoever attains cosmic consciousness loses their identity. This state of mind in which the individual phenomenon is completely dissolved is called *samadhi*.

Samadhi is divided into two stages: super consciousness and cosmic consciousness.

On the level of super-consciousness, individual awareness still exists; there is still some identification with the personality of the individual. In cosmic consciousness, however, knowing, knower and the object of knowledge become one.

The contents of the unconscious and the subconscious consist of events from our past. They lie in darkness as energy comparable with a hidden bomb that has not yet been ignited, but certainly has not been defused either. Sooner or later, the bomb will explode and exhibit its power to destroy, unless we have managed to render it harmless.

In the unconscious we store countless *karmas* from our former lives. These sleeping *karmas* can either be negative or of a divine nature. When the time is ripe, they will become active and shape our destiny.

The unconscious can be compared with a cellar beneath the house where, unbeknownst to us, many different objects have been stored. Many precious and beautiful jewels are lying there beside dangerous weapons and toxic substances. We have no knowledge of their actual location because a thick wall around the cellar prevents us from looking into this underground storeroom.

The subconscious is that part of our consciousness in which all events and actions of this lifetime are recorded. From the moment we enter our mother's womb, the subconscious becomes active and shapes our psyche. Without first clearing and purifying these parts of our consciousness we cannot develop further, because we will be held back by those *karmas*.

One of the flyers from Amnesty International depicts a small bird that is sitting on the windowsill of an open window. The bird would love to fly outside, but is held back by a heavy iron chain that is fixed around its foot. The window is open, the bird has wings with which to fly, and the desire to do so. All the necessary conditions are there, but there is one obstacle: the iron chain holds him back without mercy.

We are also chained; we are prisoners of our own *karmas*, of our own phenomenon. As long as we cannot free ourselves from this bondage, our development is blocked.

In a photograph you are able to see everything that was within the range of focus. Sometimes we discover things in the photo that we did not see before and did not want in the photo. In much the same way as a camera, our five senses impartially record everything that lies in their range of perception, whether we are conscious of it or not. The subconscious is like a computer that stores everything and the five senses are the recording instruments. Whatever reaches the unconscious, subconscious or consciousness had to be perceived by at least one or more of our senses:

The eye perceives colours and shapes.
The nose perceives smells.
The ears hear sounds.
We taste with the tongue, and
The skin perceives touch.

Through these five sense organs, we receive different impressions from the outside world. In the unconscious they are transformed into desires, longings and fears.

Most of the impressions absorbed in our daily lives do not represent a great burden to our consciousness – but some events are difficult or impossible to work through straight away. It is these that sink into our unconscious and lie there, like seeds in the ground. After some time, these seeds will begin to sprout and cause desires (VASANAS) to rise within us. Initially, these *vasanas* are unclear and not articulated, until the time they rise from the unconscious into the conscious. In the conscious mind *Buddhi*, the intellect, is active and starts to formulate, evaluate and organise these desires.

The mind is that principle within us that continuously transports impressions between the conscious and subconscious. If the mind were to rest only in the conscious, the subconscious would soon explode. It is the function of the mind to relieve the subconscious by bringing the stored contents to consciousness as quickly as possible. If we block this process it can lead to a psychic imbalance resulting in various psychosomatic diseases such as depression, nervousness, insomnia, schizophrenia, allergies and even cancer.

Each attempt to suppress the mind creates disease. The mind is like a river. A river must flow; it cannot be stopped. If we build a dam with no allowance for overflow, either the river will flood, or the dam will break under the force of the backlog of water.

We cannot switch off our senses. It is not within our power to stop seeing, tasting or smelling. But God has given us *buddhi*, the intellect, so that we can judge the impressions and organise them. But *buddhi* is very often egotistical and weak and prefers to choose that which appears to be most comfortable option.

For this reason, we have been given another ability – VIVEKA, the power of discrimination. *Viveka* is the finest development of our intellect and the essence of all our knowledge. *Viveka* and intellect relate to each other like milk and butter. Butter is the essence of milk and is derived from milk.

In the 3rd chapter of the *Bhagavad Gita* Lord Krishna says:

> *"Before you create any Karma you should know the quality of this Karma. When you know this, you will know the result that will come from this Karma."*

Before you plant a seed, it is advisable to know what kind of seed it is, because then you will also know what kind of fruits will be harvested from it. But if you do not know what seeds you have sown, you will be surprised at the fruits that come from it.

Knowing the nature of our actions comes through *Viveka*. *Viveka* means wisdom, and wisdom will guide our life towards God. *Viveka* will make us the Master of ourselves, and through this we will then gain an overview of all the factors that influence our destiny and know how to help ourselves.

Now we have gained an understanding of the meaning of mind within our own phenomenon. The mental *kosha* (*Manomaya Kosha*) is mostly unknown to us, because we do not know what lies hidden in our unconscious.

The most successful way of controlling the mind lies in following the rules of *Yama* and *Niyama*. Practise understanding, giving, praying and your *mantra* to purify your mental phenomenon.

Our mind contains innumerable impure thoughts, but generally we do not care about them because we think that nobody knows what we are thinking. However, each thought results in a counter reaction that is directed at our own self. To think negatively means to poison your own self. Positive thinking, however, leads to the purification of the mind. Many impurities stem from past lives and we need to try to finally remove them in this life.

Even if you lack material goods or are physically unwell, it is not necessarily connected to mental suffering.

At least in your mind you can always feel rich and happy!

In principle, everyone knows how they could lead a happy life. Why are only so few successful? Because most people continually invent new arguments against their own inner conviction. Our own negative attitude is the cause of all human suffering. Until the mental phenomenon is purified, enlightenment is not possible.

The body of nourishment, the body of energy and the mental body can represent considerable obstacles in our development. We can purify these three divisions of our phenomenon through healthy nourishment, good company, a healthy environment, Yoga practices and control of our senses.

VIGYANAMAYA KOSHA

VIGYANA means science. It means all knowledge that can be learnt. *Vigyanamaya Kosha* is the sum total of all our education and studies.

The intellect contains all that we have learnt since our birth. It uses memory to store all that we have learnt and experienced.

If I show you a microphone and ask you about its function, the following mental process occurs: The question enters your consciousness. A picture of a microphone will be projected onto the screen of your consciousness through the projector of your memory and the film of the intellect. In that moment when I ask you the question, you leave your body for just a split second and come here to me. This happens very fast and without you noticing. You come here with your total consciousness and "take a photo" of the object that I am showing you. Then you return again to your intellect that looks into the archives of your memory for the meaning. If you can find the picture of the object, you will consciously recognise it and be able to name it.

But if I show you something that you have never seen before and your intellect has not yet registered it and stored it in your memory, you will not be able to name it.

This is how the intellect works and develops. It can serve as a helpful tool, but it can also become a strong obstacle to us. That is why we should always use intellect and wisdom together – *Buddhi* and *Viveka*.

ANANDAMAYA KOSHA

Ananda means happiness and bliss.

There are two kinds of happiness – one is limited and one is eternal. The happiness that is limited depends on the fulfilment of our desires. Eternal bliss, however, is completely independent of outer circumstances.

In the context of *Anandamaya Kosha* we are talking about the first type of happiness, and for this reason it is also known as the "Body of Desires". And, as it is the storehouse of our sensual impressions, which are the cause of our desires and the cause of our actions, it is also called the "Causal Body".

We carry all the *karmas* in our phenomenon[2], like a backpack.

Between objects and our senses exists an attraction, like that between a magnet and iron. Through this force our desires arise. They direct our actions and, in this way, they are the source of all our problems.

We do not just exist in empty space but within our own phenomenon, which is invisible. Five sheaths surround our *Atma*, the soul or our self – the *pranic*, mental, intellectual and causal bodies, all of which manifest in the physical body. The physical body provides us with the possibility to act and to repay our karmic debts.

Manifestation or incarnation means that the dynamo of life starts turning. Positive or negative forms of energy are created, depending upon the quality of our actions.

Negative actions cause suffering to others and us. Accidents, worries, diseases, loneliness and other misfortunes happen due to the darkness in our phenomenon, which is caused by impure thoughts, words and deeds. Good deeds, however, purify our phenomenon and influence our lives in a positive way.

---

[2] Our "Phenomenon" is the energy and radiation that surrounds us: it is the expression of our entire personality, the sum of our subtle sheaths (koshas).

In its original form, our mental energy is completely neutral. It is down to us how we influence it or use it; just like a knife, it can be used to save life or to kill.

I will give you another example:

> *When you dissolve some sugar in a glass of water you can no longer see it, but you know from the sweet taste that someone has added sugar to it. This shows that the water and the sugar have not become one. The sugar is still there; it has merely changed its form.*

A human being that has not yet attained liberation will change their form when they die, but this does not mean that oneness with the Divine has been attained.

The question is, 'why has the sugar not become one with the water?' Because it has not renounced its own quality, its own individuality; it has kept its quality of the sweetness.

For as long as you do not surrender your ego and your pride, as long as you wish to stay the person that you are now, you will continue to exist as individuals and wander through the various planes of the universe. To attain union and become one, you will have to develop the same qualities and feelings as the One you wish to unite with.

That which we call God, Truth, Love or Light is life itself. Our phenomenon is like a transparent balloon that surrounds the soul or the divine Self. This balloon has five layers – the five *koshas* of nourishment, energy, mind, intellect and desires.

The presence of the *Atma* and the influence of the outer world activate our senses and cause our actions. Mixed in with our daily actions are our positive and negative qualities even when we act with the best intention, although we are often not conscious of this.

Unfortunately poison still affects us, even when we drink it unknowingly. That means negative energy is caused through both conscious and unconscious mistakes, darkening our phenomenon.

Positive deeds, however, enlighten our phenomenon. An enlightened person is surrounded by a phenomenon of the purest light in which no more negative *karmas* exist; where only light exists, darkness has no place.

Imagine you are in a completely dark room and try to "fill" a box with darkness. No matter how carefully you seal the box, as soon as you open it in bright daylight, it will immediately be filled with light. Similarly, an enlightened person cannot be influenced by *karma* under any circumstances. That person is forever freed from it.

The best thing a person can do to enlighten their phenomenon is meditation, *mantra* and prayer.

Use your energy to do selfless work. Help others, do good, and work with love. Use your talents to write a poem, paint or say something beautiful about God. Such pure actions will lead you to enlightenment and to liberation.

When your phenomenon is completely enlightened, your light will dissolve more and more into the divine light and you will become completely one with God at the end of your life. Enlightenment, God-realisation, and Self-realisation depend completely on your own actions. For this reason, trust and follow the words of your Master, do something for your spiritual development and work on yourself.

One day Mahaprabhuji's master, Sri Devpuriji, appeared in the *ashram* in Khatu in a very frightening and angry form. The disciples trembled with fear, but Mahaprabhuji smiled and sang this *bhajan* full of love,

BACANA VALA LAGE SA ME HI JANU
"How precious are the words of my Master to me."

Beautiful words are often superficial, whereas the strict words of the Master express his deep love. Rare is the disciple that can handle the strict words without becoming unbalanced. In most disciples, the *antahkarana* is still not purified and their pride and ego remain.

Trust the words of the Master.
Do not do what I do, but do what I say.
My words are the truth.

The Atma (the Self)

BACANA VALA LAGE SA, ME HI JANU
ME HI JANU OR KO KAI BAKHANU

JAGA MITHYA SAPANE KI MAYA
MURAKHA ISA ME BHARAMA BHULAYA
ME NAHI ISI KO MANU

RAJU SARPA JYU BHARAMA BHULANA
NARA NARI YU NARAKA JHULANA
ME SACI BATA BAKHANU

BACAN CORA KO HOVE NI TIRANO
LAKH CORASI ME BHATKATA FIRANO
YU GAVE SANTA SUJANU

SATAGURU SAYABA DEVAPURI SA
PRABRAHMA PUROSHOTTAMA ISA
SVAMI DIPA KAHE SATA MANU

Only I know how precious the words of
my Gurudev are to me
How can I explain it to you?

This world is an illusion, a dream,
In which the ignorant lose themselves.
I do not understand how you can mistake
a rope for a snake,
And why people go to hell for this mistake.

I am telling you the truth; those who do not
follow the words of the Master,
Will never cross the ocean of this Maya,

And will have to continue their travels through the wheel of birth and rebirth.

This is the teaching of our Sataguru Sri Devapurisa And Mahaprabhuji says: I will follow this Guru!

It is not sufficient to talk or hear about God-realisation in order to attain it. The foundation for your spiritual development is laid through your own practice and experience.

People can experience God in two aspects, as either SAGUNA or NIRGUNA.

- *Saguna* is God in a form.
- *Nirguna* is the formless, omnipresent God.

However, for many people it is difficult to accept that God can be realised in a person.

A good comparison for this is the sun. There is only one sun whose light shines on the whole earth. The sun itself is the *saguna* aspect, representing the form. The light that we can see everywhere is the *nirguna* aspect, representing the formless.

Even though the manifested God seems to be limited by its form, God's presence is unlimited and omnipresent. Nothing exists without the presence of God. God is in everything, and everything is in God. In the universal, divine phenomenon we exist as tiny individual phenomena. Each of these phenomena has its own unique quality. The individual phenomenon[3] is

---

[3] Our "phenomenon" is the energy and radiation that surrounds us: it is the expression of our entire personality, the sum of our subtle sheaths (koshas).

like a wafer-thin, transparent balloon, in the centre of which lives the *Atma,* the Self, hidden and surrounded by the five *koshas.* The *Atma* is a tiny speck of light. It is the essence of the universal *Atma – Paramatma.*

All the water on our planet comes from the ocean and will return sooner or later to the ocean – and still we do not call a small drop of water "the ocean". When the water rises from the sea in small droplets we call it vapour or fog. After rising to the sky, we no longer call it "fog", but "cloud". In this way each physical process causes a change. But only when the droplet unites again with the ocean and its limited existence ends does it become the ocean itself.

Just as the water droplet reunites with its source, we will one day reunite with God. The *Atma* within your phenomenon is a part of God, just as the drop of water is a part of the ocean.

The quantity is irrelevant. What matters is the same quality, the same nature.

Your true Self is not your body, your feelings or your thoughts, nor is it your intellect or your personal qualities. The Self is energy and vibration. It is in continuous motion. In order to reach Self-realisation, it is necessary to overcome attachment to all personal feelings and thoughts.

Only in the perception of those who have not yet recognised God does a difference between the individual Self and God exist. God-realisation means Self-realisation. If you do not re-alise your Self, you cannot realise God. And as long as you have not realised God, you do not know who you are.

It is everyone's goal to reunite with God. We are all travellers. Whether we are conscious of it or not, everyone wishes to return to God.

The raindrop falls into the ocean. The smaller part will always return to the bigger part, as the child returns to the mother. The force of attraction that is in operation between them is love – and it is love that will return us to God. We are all searching for our Self. Even though our Self is always within us, until we can recognise this it seems as if we have lost it.

> *A Yogi sat under a tree, meditating. A farmer joined him to keep him company. He asked the Yogi, "Do you know why I joined you?"*
> *The Yogi shook his head.*
> *"When I saw you sitting by yourself, I thought that you must feel lonely."*
> *"On the contrary," replied the Yogi, "it is now that I am lonely. Before I was with God."*

This is how the events of the outer world at times separate us from our true inner union.

The way our phenomenon works can be compared with a dynamo that produces two kinds of energy – negative and positive.

The negative energy is created by bad thoughts, which darken our phenomenon. Darkness means ignorance. Through good *karmas* – *mantra* practice, prayer, meditation, being loving, forgiving, helping others and selfless service – we can purify ourselves. Such deeds enlighten our phenomenon. If the essence of a person is guided totally by positive and divine qualities only, his phenomenon becomes completely enlightened. Such a person is an "enlightened" one, one who is united with God. For God is love, light, harmony, knowing, reality, truth and union.

However, in those people who, out of ignorance, align themselves with darkness, will form corresponding dark qualities. As a consequence, they will suffer from accidents, disease, problems and many other difficulties. They wander through the universe in darkness and will continue to be reborn again and again.

Samadhi is the union of knowing, knower and object. The object is God. The knowing is the recognition of God. The knower is the *Atma.*

Knowledge of the truth is Divine knowledge. It is light and love, without any lack of clarity, without any shadow. Such a Yogi achieves liberation, *Moksha,* enlightenment and Self-realisation. Their individual consciousness opens to the Universal Being. No longer do they strive for *siddhis*, miraculous powers, because they already have everything. They are not searching for miracles anymore, as they have recognised what an amazing miracle it is to be born as a human and to be alive – to be able to see, hear, speak and act. They understand that the greatest miracle of all consists in being granted the blessing to realise God.

Our Self is our *Guru,* our Self is our disciple. Our Self is our friend and our Self is our enemy. Learn from yourself. Watch, analyse, understand, accept, realise and love your Self; then you will realise your Self.

A man was thirsty and was desperately searching for water. Finally, he came to a creek and bent over the water to drink. While bending over, he lost his balance and fell headlong into the water. The man was so delighted that he had at long last found the water he had been longing for that he was not at all worried about the loss of balance. He surrendered himself happily to the flowing of the water.

We all are thirsty for Divine wisdom. Even though we have already lived forever in God's consciousness, we are not yet able to recognise this at our current level of consciousness.

Yoga in Daily Life® can show us the way to this recognition. Nobody can simply give you liberation and Self-realisation; practice, experience and *Guru Bhakti* are needed.

Feel free, especially free of fear. Fear is the most terrible pain that exists within us. With the grace of God, we are able to overcome even the greatest of our fears. *Mahaprabhuji*, our *Gurudeva*, is guiding and protecting us. He helps us overcome all difficulties.

The Meaning of Life

To be born as a human being is the greatest of good fortune, a blessing that is extremely precious and rare. For this reason, one should not waste one's life. The purpose of human life is to do good and to achieve God-realisation. Blessed and lucky are those who do good for others and for themselves. Anyone who is not doing this is wasting precious time.

Make a decision that from now on you will use every minute of your life for the good.

To be able to do good, firstly we need to have good health. A healthy body and a healthy mind produce good thoughts, and good thoughts lead to good actions. For this reason, the first goal of Yoga in Daily Life® is to achieve a stable and balanced state of health. This does not mean only physical health; it also includes mental, emotional, social and spiritual health.

Our body is not immortal. One day it will be taken from us again. We cannot keep the body forever, but the *Atma* is immortal.

Today we live in a highly technical civilization, in an era of "science". Many people believe more in modern science than in religion. However, there is already scientific proof that there is life after death.

It is not "you" who dies, but merely your body.

After death you are able to review your whole life. Just like on a movie screen, pictures of each stage of your life, from childhood to the last minutes of your life, will pass in front of you. You will see everything. You will remember the happy and the sad feelings, and you will relive them all again. This is the proof that these experiences and feelings cannot be located in the physical body; they occur at another level of consciousness.

On German television, I once saw an interview with an American scientist, Dr. Moody. He has done research into the experiences of people who were clinically dead and were revived. Some of these people recalled what they had experienced while they were outside their bodies. They remembered how they left their physical body in their astral body. In this state they no longer had any sensations of physical pain. Without emotion or suffering they were able to see their own body as it was lying at the scene of the accident or on the operating table. Some of them reported that they had gone through a tunnel and could see a brilliant light at the end of it. This light guided them further on into other planes where they met their relatives and friends who had passed away before them.

The teachings of Yoga tell us about three such tunnels: IDA, PINGALA and SUSHUMNA. Going through *Pingala* will take you to the light. *Ida* will take you to the darkness. Whoever leaves through *Sushumna* will attain liberation – but this is only possible for the Self-realised person.

At the moment of death, different experiences are possible. It is possible that one is torn away violently by the god of death (*Yama*). His appearance is horrific like that of a devil. Those who have created much bad *karma* for themselves will have this experience (the Christian teachings also tell us that you will go to hell, meaning to the devil, as a consequence of your sins). Others, however, experience the transition to the other plane as soft and gentle, and their ancestors expect them and receive them. And some will even receive a joyful welcome by an angelic, heavenly Light form.

But how is it possible to be received by one's ancestors when there is rebirth? How come the ancestors are still in the other world? This is because it can take a very long time before you have another opportunity to be reborn. Sometimes the great fortune can occur that one is suddenly liberated when a member of the family becomes Self-realised. In this moment, seven generations of ancestors and seven generations of descendants will be liberated. The light of Self-realisation has such a powerful radiation that everyone who is slightly connected to this light will also be liberated.

It is dependent upon each and every one of us what we achieve in this life.

Each one of you has to know for yourself what life means to you and what your goal in life is. Yoga gives us the possibility of achieving the goal in this lifetime. It would be a terrible shame if you were to die without reaching your goal. It is possible that you will be born again as a human in your next life, but it is far from a certainty. The opportunity of a human life is not received too often. Nobody knows what the next day, or even the next hour will bring. For this reason, it is important to use each moment very consciously.

In a soccer game you have twenty-two players and one ball. The ball belongs to nobody. Anyone can grab it and shoot a goal. In the same way, we are all players in the game of life. If you play this game with concentration, consciousness, honesty and fairness you will hit the ball into the goal of liberation.

Try to understand the purpose of life. Recognise why you are born and make the right decision!

A hunter, about to venture into the forest, came across a Yogi. When he saw the Saint, he hid the gun behind his back and tried to pass him quickly, but the Yogi stopped him and asked, "What are you hiding from me?"

"Nothing," replied the hunter.

"Do not lie! You are keeping something hidden!"

"Master, please forgive me! It is a gun. But I am only going hunting out of the necessity to feed my family. I am a poor man and do not know any other way."

The Yogi replied, "In your last life you killed many animals and because of that bad Karma you have created your poverty in this life. You think only of your children, but not of the poor children of the animals that you are killing. Animals feel the same love for their young ones as people do. These innocent animals have done nothing to you, do not kill them!"

"But from where will I get my food?" the hunter asked the Yogi despairingly.

The Yogi answered him, "I will help you. See this stone? It is a Paras stone that will change iron into gold. If you touch a piece of iron with this stone it will immediately turn into gold. I will leave the stone with you for seven days. You can make as much gold as you wish with this stone, but I will take it back from you after seven days."

Overjoyed, the hunter thanked him and rushed home.

The next morning, he went to the market and asked for the price of iron.

"One hundred rupees for a kilo," the iron trader answered. The hunter enquired further, "Do you think the iron will be cheaper in the next few days?" They replied, "Possibly, come back tomorrow."

The hunter decided that it was better to wait and went home without buying any. Sure enough, the price for iron had gone down the next day and the traders assured him that it would go down even further. Each day passed and

*the hunter would go to the market, still waiting for the
iron to become even cheaper.*

*On the seventh day, however, the Yogi appeared in front
of the hunter's hut and demanded his stone back. The
hunter was shocked and said, "But I have not yet used it.
Please leave it with me another day!"*

*But the Yogi shook his head. "You had a whole week to get
yourself as much gold as you wanted. Now the time and
your chance have passed and I will take the stone back
again!"*

Like this *Paras* stone, you have received the "golden opportunity" in this life of being a human. Do not wait! Do not waste
your time. Practise Yoga and recognise the meaning of your
life now!

Choose God

To make a choice means to renounce other possibilities at the same time. Without renunciation, no real decision can be made.

It is better not to make sudden decisions, especially if you are in an emotional state of mind. Take your time and think deeply until you have become completely clear about any possible consequences that could arise from your venture. However, once you have made your decision, stick to your choice under all circumstances.

Mahaprabhuji said, "When the waves are high, do not dive for pearls." So, wait until the waves of your emotions have calmed down and then make your choice; utilise both the heart and the intellect when you are no longer affected by your emotions.

The strongest power within us is *Atma Bal* – the inner will of the *Atma.* By making your choice for the *Atma*, your consciousness will become clear and free.

It would be a terrible shame to miss the purpose of your life! We often receive the opportunity for a new start – to make changes in our profession, our place of residence or our circle of friends. A lifetime in human form, however, can be a one-off chance in eons, and we do not know when such a favourable constellation will come again.

Once the chain is broken, it is too late. Time is justice. Time does not wait. Nobody enjoys its protection. If we realise this after our death, we will ask imploringly to receive another chance to make up for what we missed. But how can we know if anyone is listening to our request? Maybe God does not exist in the way we imagine Him?

For that reason, it is very important to worship the divine within a person; to worship the Divine consciousness manifested in human form, to follow and to surrender to that person. The divine power that has embodied itself in this Divine incarnation will help and guide us.

If we wish to achieve something in our worldly affairs, we will turn to someone who has influence or wealth. And similarly, simply speaking our desires into space will most likely not bring the desired results. It is for this reason that we turn to the divine incarnations with our prayers. They are the reigning personalities within the universe who radiate a strong and far reaching power of attraction. By putting ourselves under their protection, our astral being will be safely guided to the light.

Blinded by intellectual doubts, false pride and egoism, some people do not accept that God can also appear to us in human form as a person. They only want to accept the formless, omnipresent aspect of God – its *nirguna* form. But this is just as silly as refusing to take in the nourishment that forms the basis of our continuing existence in this body. Surely there is some reason why we are born into a body made of matter, into a material world? For this reason, we should not reject God in His physical form.

If we just sit there and meditate into nothingness, there is no purpose and it only wastes time and energy, just as if we were to pour oil into the sand. It is better if our meditation is directed specifically to a certain goal or object, toward a task or an image.

At this moment we exist as individuals, and will remain as such unless we unite with one such extraordinary person whom we recognise as a Divine Incarnation.

Just as the influence of the president of a country reaches the whole country, the mercy of a Divine Incarnation, such as Mahaprabhuji, Jesus, Krishna, Rama and others, extends throughout the whole universe. They are the "Kings of Heaven". Just as the president rules over his country, the "King of Heaven" guides the whole cosmos.

Who is the "King of Heaven"? The God incarnate! He can liberate us. He can give us everything. We call him God, or the *Guru* principle *(Guru-tattva)*. It is important that we make a clear choice of one ISHTA DEVATA (God manifested in a Divine Incarnation) whom we personally revere. Until we have made this decision, the gate of God-realisation will not open for us.

You have already decided on Yoga and your *mantra*. Now it is important that you stick with it!

I pray every day to Mahaprabhuji, Sri Devpuriji, Holy Guruji and to all Saints, that they may protect my disciples and direct their spiritual development onto the right path. Wherever I may be, my prayers and my best wishes are always with you.

Pray and Meditate

Without prayer and meditation, life is empty and without purpose.

Every day that you miss your prayer and meditation is a day lost.

Working and eating are actions that are part of the natural law. These activities are not only a part of human life, but they are also a characteristic of all living beings, and even of matter itself. But human beings have an additional task – to pray and to meditate.

Meditation should be a deep need within us. We should crave it as much as an addict craves his drug. A heavy smoker will never forget his cigarette and will always find time for it. When you have missed your meditation, you should miss it like a chain smoker would miss his cigarette.

We should dedicate two hours each day to our spiritual practice. We suffer from delusion if we pretend that we do not have the time for that. We simply waste too much time on other things so that we do not find the space for the most important thing in our life – our own spiritual development.

There are twenty-four hours a day at our disposal. If we take eight hours out for both sleeping and working, we still have another eight hours for other activities. We should divide this time in such a way that we keep at least two hours for our practice. Without our daily practice and discipline, there will be no success. Our spiritual treasury will gradually empty unless we regularly refill it with our practice.

We need to make a clear decision about what we wish to achieve in our life and then steadfastly stick to this decision. There are, however, two things we need to avoid under all circumstances – competition and provocation. Competitive thinking is created when we act with the goal of gaining something. If one wants to win, another automatically has to lose. Such a challenge is fed by ego and pride – signs of great ignorance – which will act like a wall and block the path of a spiritual seeker.

This is the opposite of spiritual principles. The best path to spirituality is devotion and helping others. First grant to another what you would want for yourself. But remember, all your thoughts, words and deeds have as much of an effect on you as they do on others. Each action is automatically followed by a corresponding reaction. Work on yourself and follow your path slowly but steadily. Learn from everything that you encounter in your life.

For example, you can learn from a tree. A tree is not attached to the one who planted it, nor will it take vengeance on the one who throws a stone at it. Just the opposite; it will even give sweet fruits to that person, and give shade and protection to everyone who seeks refuge under it. Even though it bows to a stronger power and bends in a storm, it will hold onto its roots and remain steadfast and immovable in its place.

To clarify the position of a spiritual seeker, the following image is useful:

Imagine yourself standing in the middle of a circle from which several pathways exit in a star like fashion. You want to reach a certain goal, and contemplate which of the paths will lead you there. Each path is inviting in its own beauty and has its own character. One leads through meadows rich with flowers, one through the forest, and another over sunny hillsides. But you know that you have only a certain time to make your decision and to walk your chosen path.

Your goal is at the end of the path. As long as a river flows it remains a river. Once it joins the ocean, it becomes the ocean. That means that for as long as a path exists, realisation has not been achieved.

Now turn your point of view around and see the goal exactly where you are standing, not far away from yourself. This means that rather than leading away from you, the paths lead towards you. Now you need not follow a path that leads you away from the centre, because what you are looking for is exactly where you are!

Do not pray, "Lord! Let me come to you". Rather, cry, "Please come to me, oh Lord!" God can be with you so much faster than you are able to reach him.

All paths lead to one goal – and this goal lies within you. It lies in your heart, in your soul, in your *Atma*. The different paths symbolise the striving of your senses and emotions, which can be directed either outward or inward. To meditate means to go within oneself, not to run away from oneself. For this reason, direct your feelings to your innermost core and open your heart.

The one who has been proven guilty lands in prison because he has acted against the law. The liberator, however, only visits the prison to show the prisoner the path to freedom. To people outside of the prison, it may appear that both are imprisoned because they cannot differentiate between the liberator and the prisoner.

72

We are all born into this world as prisoners of our own *karmas*. *Gurudeva* incarnates as a liberator on this earth to redeem us. God appears in the same form as us in order to speak to us in our own language and to guide us. For the benefit of his devotees he will go through all the comfortable and uncomfortable conditions of life and surrender himself voluntarily to all the biological processes of life. God will take all of this upon himself to liberate humans. His love for all creatures is immeasurable.

Do not think negatively but lead a harmonious life. Negative thoughts poison your whole phenomenon. Stay on the spot where God has put you. He will pick you up from exactly there and guide you further.

Take this life as an opportunity to finally attain liberation. Ask yourself: "What is the reason for my being here? What is my goal?" The answer lies within you, and you will come to experience it in meditation. Realise your inner wisdom, your inner light.

Honour your Master and be grateful that he has awakened you from your sleep of ignorance. A clear and pure relationship with your Master is one of the main pillars for your spiritual development. Express your gratitude to Him in your love for all living beings and live with *Sant Bhava* in this world. With devotion, prayer and meditation you will reach your goal!

Prayer

Prayer is a personal consultation with God.

The impossible, the unreachable and the unimaginable can all be achieved through prayer.

To illustrate this, I will to tell about an event that actually happened.

> In Kansas City (USA) there lived a family in which the father suffered from a bad disease that, despite a lot of effort and medical treatment, could not be cured. One day a friend advised him to travel to India in order to learn how to pray. Surely, he could be helped through prayer, the friend reckoned.
>
> So, the couple undertook the long and tiresome journey to India by train and boat, because at that time aeroplanes did not exist. In India they learnt to pray and within several weeks the very sick man was healed. His prayer had helped him.
>
> After his return to Kansas City he decided to learn Sanskrit and open an Institute in which prayer was taught.
>
> The name of the man was Max Mueller. He became well known in America, as well as in Europe. He was the first American to translate the holy Vedas into English.
>
> Max Mueller was convinced by his own miraculous recovery that anything could be achieved through prayer.
>
> One day he received further proof of the miraculous power of prayer. The spiritual school he had founded was run as a charitable, non-profit organization and money and provisions were running low. On one particular day two hundred people had turned up to be fed, double the

number they had expected. The cooks were desperate because there was not sufficient food to cook for all the people, and no money to buy any more food.

Max Mueller did not want to send away the hungry people who had come full of expectations. He told the cooks to ring the bell at lunchtime as usual. "Trust in God and pray," he ordered the cooks. He himself retired into his room and prayed ardently to God to help so that these people would not be disappointed.

When the time came for lunch, the cooks asked Max Mueller again what they should do. In the meantime, even more people had arrived and it appeared that surely there would not be enough food for all. "Ring the bell," was the firm reply.

At that very moment, a truck stopped outside the institute with food for three hundred people already prepared. The driver explained to Max Mueller that the delivery had been planned for a big party that had to be cancelled at the last minute. The organizer had decided to donate the food to a charitable organization. In this way, the plates of all the people waiting in the institute were overflowing with the finest morsels.

Many prayers come from people who are suffering, many from loving hearts and many from seekers filled with spiritual longing. The true prayer, however, comes from one who is Self-realised. God lives in every heart. All living beings are creatures of one creator, and the Realised one feels his Self in all living beings.

Once a hungry fox was looking for food. He found a coconut. However, he could not open it. He wanted to give up and keep going, but the sweet smell followed him and made him return to try and break open the strong shell yet again.

There are many people who want to know who or what is God, but, just as the coconut was to the fox, God is an unexplored mystery to them. In order to enjoy the coconut, it first has to be opened. In the same way, to experience God's blessing, the heart of the human must open first. People try again and again to reach God, and give up and move away, only to return. Fortunately, there are techniques like those in Yoga that can help us to reach our goal.

Have faith in God and pray to God. Not only should you hear and read about God, you also need to realise God. If you believe you know what is God, but have only heard or read about God, then you are like the fox that has sniffed the coconut but not yet opened it.

Prayer and meditation lead to realisation.

Mahatma Gandhi said, *"Physically I can fast for many days, spiritually I cannot fast at all. My spiritual nourishment is my prayer."*

Mahatma Gandhi's thoughts, spirit and will were very strong. What gave him this power? His prayers and his practice. Whenever you encounter any difficulties, retreat into your inner temple and pray. Your prayer needs to come from your heart.

There are auspicious times for prayer: in the early morning before your daily routine begins, and in the evening just before sunset. At sunrise the consciousness awakens. The whole of nature awakens at the time of dawn, and at dusk it retreats again. The only exception is humans, who often feel lazy in the morning and restless in the evening.

A saint said, *"Oh human, if you do not contemplate God, you are less than the animals. After their death at least, their bones and skins can be used. However, what value has the life of a human who does not live his life according to God's will."*

Give your love, help, protection, understanding and forgiveness. If you wish to follow the teachings of Jesus, think of the words that he spoke on the cross, *"Forgive them Father for they know not what they do."*

Follow the principle of *Ahimsa* (non-violence) toward both people and animals. It is the highest principle, a divine principle.

Do not miss the golden opportunity to be able to live on this planet as a human being. This is a very rare opportunity. Who knows when or if it will be offered to you again? For this reason, it would be a shame to waste your life!

Heaven and hell both exist here on earth. Try to fulfil your destiny, for that is the essence of this life. No matter what vehicle you use to reach your goal, the main thing is that you get there. Once you have reached your goal you can put your vehicle away as you will no longer need it. No matter which religion or which path you follow, its only purpose is to lead you to your goal.

All rivers terminate once they reach the ocean. Once you begin to live with the truth you will not need a path anymore. But until you have reached your goal, keep going and keep using one of your most important tools: prayer.

Commentary on a Bhajan by Holy Guruji

ABA HAMA GURU SARANA SUKHA PAYA
SAGARA LAHRE SAMAYA

Now I am happy with my Gurudeva
Finally, the wave has become one with the ocean!

The individual Self is part of the Divine Self, just as the wave is part of the ocean. In reality, the wave and the ocean are one and the same. The only difference lies in the quantity, not in the essence. Just as the waves have reunited with the ocean, so have I reunited with my *Gurudeva*.

GYAN GHATA LE SATAGURU AYA
AMRITA JALA BARASAYA
AMRITA NIRA PIYA MANA BHARAKA
NIRBHAYA NE CALA THAYA

The knowledge of the Satguru is infinite.

Mahaprabhuji's words were like heavenly ambrosia for the people, like life-giving rain for the dried-up vegetation.

I have drunk this nectar till my mind was totally filled
with it
Through this nectar of wisdom, I am now without fear
And have reached the end of my search.

Those who are searching are restless and wander around until they have found the goal. Those who have become one have come to rest. They are as immovable as the sky upon which the clouds are moving.

PARASA HE GURUDEVA HAMARA
LOKA KANCANA KARAYA
SOHAM SABDA DIYA SARAVA ME
KOVA HANSA BANAYA

My Gurudev is the Paras stone
Through which iron is transformed into gold.
He gave me the mantra SO HAM
And transformed the crow into a swan.

ANANT JANAMA CORASI BHOGI
MARA YAMO KI KHAYA
GURUDEVA YAMA DANDA CHURAYA
LEKHA PURA KARAYA

Countless lives I wandered from death to rebirth
How often was I tortured by Yama, the god of death!

The process of death and rebirth is not easy. We have all been through this experience many times, only we have forgotten it.

Gurudeva freed me from the punishment of Yama
By ridding me of all my karmic debts.

Through each *Karma,* more *Karma* will come. Each action causes a reaction. This chain of cause and effect can only be broken by the *Gurudeva.*

AGE JANAMA ANEKA GAMAYA
GURU BINA BHEDA NA PAYA
PAYA BHEDA KHEDA SABA MIT GAYA
URA BICA BHANA UGAYA

79

Before I met my Guru I wasted many lives
The mystery of life was hidden from me
When I recognised the mystery, all
my suffering finally dissolved
In my heart the sun was rising and all
the darkness of ignorance disappeared.

Guru Nanak says in a poem, *"And even if a hundred suns and moons would rise – the darkness of ignorance in your heart can only be removed by the grace of Gurudeva."*

SRI PUJYA BHAGAVAN DIPA DAYALU
BEHADA HANSA PATHAYA
KAHE MADHAVANANDA ANANDA HE
JANAM SARANA NAI AYA

Sri Mahaprabhuji liberated countless souls
He also guided my soul into the infinite
Now I am one with all. Infinite and limitless I live in eternal bliss
For neither death nor rebirth exist for me anymore.

How is it that we cannot realise this? It is because we have not yet discovered the mystery.

You are able to find the key to this mystery when you realise *Gurudeva* within yourself. Until then you only circle around reality in your search for it. Remove any lack of clarity and doubts; otherwise you will not be successful. Until you have found certainty, you are still searching.

Hindu Dharm Samrat Paramhans Swami Madhavanandaji

Mahaprabhuji said in a *bhajan*,

GURU SA BINA KARAJA NAY SARE
Without Gurudeva you will not be successful.

You may try countless techniques and think of countless theories, but your search will remain fruitless because you cannot cross the ocean of ignorance this way. You may wander to every place of pilgrimage and renounce the world, but without the *Gurudeva* you will not reach your goal.

Mahaprabhuji said,

"I feel sorry for all those who renounce the world because they long for reality, for as long as they are without a Master they will remain in ignorance."

Many people worship statues and pictures in blind faith, even though they would be better off searching for a living Master and then serving Him. A person in whom the pride of the ego is dominant will refuse to bow to a Master. It is easier for him to bow down to a statue.

Try to recognise reality, otherwise your life passes without purpose and who knows what will await you afterwards?

Regrettably, only a few recognise the golden opportunity that their life offers. It is as if you hold a diamond in your hand without recognising its value. Whoever knows the significance of a jewel will treat it with respect and will look after it carefully. Whoever does not know the difference between a diamond and a piece of glass might throw it into the garbage bin at the next opportunity.

You may throw away all your bad habits and doubts, but not your precious life. A negative intellect and weaknesses within your character pose huge obstacles on your path. Be clear about your goal! Ignorance brings only suffering to people. Without knowledge there is no liberation!

Whoever recognises this will be successful. Those who do not recognise this throw their life away.

Mahaprabhuji said:

"Until you give your body and mind over unconditionally into the service of Gurudeva in order to carry on the divine light, you will be unable to reach realisation and you will be unable to completely purify yourself and be reunited."

During Mahaprabhuji's long lifetime, countless people visited his *satsangs,* but only a few of them truly understood Him. Of thousands of disciples only a small number could realise Him: for example, Mangilalji, Brahmanandaji, Lalanandaji and Holy Guruji. The story of their lives and realisation is written in Sri Mahaprabhuji's biography "Lila Amrit".

The disciple who has devoted his life totally to *Gurudeva* cannot be stopped by anything or anyone in the whole universe. He moves in the Divine Light, without obstacles or *karmic* barriers.

Asanas

Asana means place. Your Yoga mat is your *asan*, where you are sitting is your *asan*. It is simply a place where one can sit and be comfortable.

Another meaning of *asana* is to keep the body still for a while in a comfortable position. Your relaxing posture, for example, is called *Anandasana*, the lotus posture is called *Padmasana*, and *Sukhasana* is a comfortable sitting posture.

All living beings have their own way of lying or sitting. There are 8.4 million kinds of living beings, and as just as many *asanas*. Many of the *asanas* imitate the postures of animals, who move in a natural and relaxed manner.

Two worlds exist side by side and are woven into each other. One is without fault – this perfect world is created by God. The other world, shaped by humans, is full of mistakes and out of balance. Due to wrong ideas, people today lead very unnatural lives.

As a result of this, the human being has become the un-happiest, sickest, most aggressive, most suffering and restless of all living beings. And yet still man calls himself the most intelligent and most highly developed being. But ever since mankind separated itself from God and nature this, unfortunately, is no longer true.

Through practicing the *asanas* that have been adapted from nature, we have the opportunity of regaining our natural health and harmony.

The scriptures tell us that we can avoid reincarnating into a particular animal form by practicing certain *asanas*. That is why *asanas* have names relating to specific animals to help us erase karmic attributes of a particular species.

It has been shown that we can overcome certain characteristics through practising specific *asanas*. For example, when a cobra feels aggressive it will raise its upper body, and as it calms down it will again lower itself. So, going into the Cobra (*Bhujangasana*) for a few minutes has a calming effect.

Asanas have a positive influence on the mind, intellect, emotions and physical functions, as well as on our *karmas*. They also have a balancing effect on our *chakras* (energy centres) and *nadis* (energy channels), and give us renewed energy.

Asanas can be practiced in two ways. The position can either be held statically for some time, or it can be practised dynamically in rhythm with the breath.

Asanas are important for a healthy body. A healthy body is important for healthy thoughts. Healthy thoughts are important for healthy deeds, and healthy deeds are important for a healthy society and environment.

It is beneficial for a practitioner to know the original names of the *asanas*. As already mentioned with *Bhujangasana,* the names have a close connection to the effects of the practice.

Asanas need to be done in a certain order; for example, one posture is followed by an appropriate counter posture. If you practice according to the system of Yoga in Daily Life® and follow its rules, the *asanas* will lead you to perfect health and bring you back into union with your inner nature.

Prana is lost with each physical movement. You can tell how much energy you have used by the extent of your physical tiredness. With relaxation and rest, fresh *prana* streams into the body so that it can recover again. The more *prana* that has been expended, the more rest time is required. If, however, you relax with the help of YOGA NIDRA, the "sleep of the Yogi", regeneration happens very quickly.

Prana (life energy) is continuously flowing through our body. *Prana* is pure, neutral energy, without specific qualities, which expands freely and independently throughout the whole universe. Where there is energy, there is movement. Movement means development and growth. Growth means life. Growth and movement can only exist where there is energy.

In the universe a continuous change and exchange of elements takes place. Where something is added, something else needs to give way and vice versa. If you fill a container with water, the air inside will be removed at the same time, and when you empty the container the air will immediately stream back inside.

Our body is full of waste products. These are substances whose energy has been used up and are now harmful to the body. Our body resembles a house with many windows. Through these windows, fresh air streams into the house continuously and replenishes the old used air inside. When breathing in we renew our life force, and when breathing out, old stale substances are removed.

Even the smallest movement uses energy. When doing sports, you lose a lot of energy. Just think how an athlete looks after competition: usually completely out of breath and exhausted. Through the movement required in performing the *asanas* we also lose energy, but we regain far more energy from the *asanas* than we lose. Practising *asanas* dissolves energy blockages and gives us new strength at the same time. When the body is enriched with positive energy, all physical functions work more harmoniously and we feel well and healthy.

A healthy body creates a healthy mind. A healthy mind creates healthy thoughts. And out of healthy thoughts come "healthy" and right actions. The right actions in turn create health-promoting reactions in body and mind. Out of that a sense of inner contentment is achieved – *SANTOSHA*.

That is why it is so important to practice *asanas*.

The body is the temple of the soul. Always preserve its purity. Pure nourishment, pure thoughts, pure feelings, pure words, prayer, *mantra* and meditation are the means for this.

Mantra

Your *mantra* is your constant companion. It protects you on your spiritual path at the astral level. Through the *mantra* even those *karmas* that you are not aware of and cannot perceive are purified.

The *mantra* becomes your spiritual breath.

As the breath preserves your body, the *mantra* preserves your *Atma*.

But *mantra* repetition on its own is not enough. It is also necessary to strive for a deep connection with your Master. Realise your Master within you!

We devote our *Mantra* practice to Mahaprabhuji and Sri Devpuriji.

The words of the Master are *Guru vakya.*

All holy books contain *Guru vakya*, the words of God-realised people. This means they are the words of God. Each of these words contains a deeper meaning, which is not immediately understood by most people. But a time will come when everyone will recognise the power and meaning in the words of the Master.

The Master-disciple tradition has existed since time immemorial. The Bible is actually a dialogue between Master and disciple.

Even animals have their masters from whom they learn. The young ones imitate the grown-up members of their species, who become their teachers. In the same way, parents are the first masters for their children, their friends the second, their schoolteachers the third, and the priest the fourth. The fifth master is the spiritual Master, the *Satguru*, and the final, sixth master is your own Self.

The Master is like a burning candle, lighting the candle of the disciple. When the candle of the disciple is finally lit, it has the same function and quality as the Master's candle. Until then, however, hard work, patience, discipline and regular ongoing practice are required.

Yoga in Daily Life® gives you a complete and perfect system in which you can be sure to reach your goal.

At first, your *mantra* serves to calm and harmonise your psyche and to improve your capacity to concentrate. But its true purpose is to lead you to enlightenment and God-realisation.

Practice your *mantra* continually and take your spirituality seriously. Keep in mind that you are a seeker who wishes to reach their goal. Yoga is what you have been seeking for a very long time, either consciously or subconsciously.

All my words already exist in you. Nothing is truly new to you. As you hear my words, three kinds of reactions can occur. You may merely be conscious of what I am saying, or my words remind you of something, or they awaken a deep longing for the Truth within you.

All knowledge is slumbering within you. The words of the Master and the Holy Scriptures help to awaken your sleeping consciousness and bring your hidden knowledge to the light.

I once saw a scientific documentary on television about the workings of the human brain during conscious and unconscious actions. One person was given some glasses, through which she saw everything upside down. The whole world stood on its head. In the beginning this person was not even capable of standing up or walking. But after two weeks she was used to the glasses and this upside-down world. She moved about feeling completely normal and secure. These experiments proved that 99% of all our movements happen unconsciously and habitually. If a person is confronted with a new or very different situation, initially they go into psychic and physical confusion and will then need time to adapt and change.

Exactly the same thing occurs when our sleeping consciousness is woken too suddenly and quickly: the experience of other planes of consciousness that we are not accustomed to will disturb our equilibrium. For this reason, even though it is beneficial to promote the development of our consciousness, it is best not to rush, and to instead allow the development to unfold at a slow and natural pace.

Many of my disciples would like to have spiritual experiences and astral travelling. However, if they suddenly feel themselves leaving their body and looking at it from the outside, they become scared and cannot handle this new situation.

Why do they get scared? Because they are afraid that something could happen to them and they will lose themselves.

For this reason, you need to continue slowly and steadily on your path and practise your *mantra* with devotion.

Try to understand your Master. We all have a very deep connection with each other. Love, friendship and respect bind us together. This connection is indescribable and can only be felt in the heart. Nourish this subtle spiritual bond carefully, and don't destroy it with intellectual doubts and complexes.

To receive a *mantra* means to take a step into the Light. With the *mantra* initiation, the purification of your *karmas* begins. It is a long process supported by mutual trust.

Your *mantra* is your constant companion, your true protector, and your friend. When accompanied by your *mantra* you will always be happy wherever you are, in this physical world or in the astral world, on this planet or another. Of course, firstly you have to reach the stage where the *mantra* unfolds within you and becomes effective, and this only occurs with constant practice.

When you are starving, nothing else exists in your consciousness except the thought of food. When you have an over-powering longing for God, your whole consciousness becomes filled through and through with God.

Birth and death are part of a cyclic process. We can easily see this happening in nature. However, in the cycle of the elements it is uncertain if a dead leaf will return to be part of the same tree. The path of the leaf may take a completely different course. Similarly, the soul is not connected to a specific form. It can reincarnate into other forms.

Some people are of the opinion that human consciousness is so highly evolved that we will never come back in animal form. This assumption is based on a serious misjudgement caused by pure pride and egotistical thinking. Those people in their arrogance no longer perceive the laws of nature and the cosmos.

Sure enough, every drop of water will eventually reach the sea. However, this can take a very long time, depending on where it falls and which route it takes. It can fall on a street, a meadow, a mountain or a lake and also into a river which flows directly into the ocean.

The ocean is the symbol of universal God consciousness. The drops are the individuals. Sooner or later all drops will surely return to the ocean.

Your *mantra* is your way to God.

Discourse for the Kriya Initiation

The advanced Yoga technique of *kriya* is the most effective method of purifying us of our *karmas*. *Kriyas* exert a far-reaching effect on our subconscious and unconscious mind. Much of what has been dormant within us will be drawn out and resolved, often even unnoticed by us.

There are plenty of obstacles on our path, like boulders blocking our way. We need to have inner strength to be able to overcome these barriers. The road leading to our goal can be long and difficult. We must have clarity about what we wish to achieve to avoid missing the path.

There are three basic principles necessary on the spiritual path:

- *BHAKTI – devotion to God*
  Devotion only exists where there is trust.
  Devotion means to give of yourself, and once given not to ask for it back.

- *GYANA – knowledge and clarity*
  Be one-pointed and unwavering in removing every thought or feeling that lacks clarity so that you can make decisions with a clear consciousness.

- *ABHYASA – Devotional practice*
  Your practice is the tool handed to you by your Master. Honour it, use it and continue your practice faithfully.

As it says in one prayer,

> *Oh Lord! Let me never forget your name!*
> *May it always resound in my heart.*
> *Oh Lord Krishna*
> *May you stand before me at the end of my life*
> *And may the sound of your flute draw my soul towards*
> *you.*
> *May I find liberation through this very sound!*

May your *mantra* be your last words on this planet. Wherever your last thoughts turn at the end of your life is where your path will continue.

All of us are sitting together in a boat, and only the future will show who has held on until we reach the goal. It may be that the Captain will change. Who knows how much longer my body will be able to accompany you? What truly matters is that you stay in Mahaprabhuji's boat until the end of the journey. You must be completely purified of all doubts in order to realise Mahaprabhuji.

You have yet to go through many more experiences in your life. This *maya* is powerful and appears in many different forms. Be steadfast and do not change your path. Everyone in life is confronted with countless difficulties and problems, and sometimes we think that we cannot go on. Keep your goal in mind and have full faith in Mahaprabhuji, who is guiding you. Allow your love to grow with each step. After death, things that seemed to be so important at the time no longer matter.

When a disciple comes to me saying that they feel pulled in another direction, I do not say much and am very careful with my advice. When *Maya* attacks it can be as dangerous as a hungry lion. If you give it what it wants, it will tear you apart.

Practicing your *kriya* develops your discipline. The practice purifies your unconscious mind and leads you more quickly towards the goal. Through *kriya* an uninterrupted purification process takes place in our subconscious and unconscious, without us even noticing.

Many disciples start to doubt their Yoga path when, despite their regular practice, they become sick. However, you can never measure your spiritual progress by the health of your physical body. The body is bound by the laws of nature and is in a continual state of flux. Even a Yogi rarely dies without physical disease.

Why, for example, has Holy Guruji been suffering with many physical ailments? Because it is sometimes difficult for the physical body to withstand the enormous power of the spiritual energy flowing into it.

Often, people who follow the spiritual path will be affected more frequently than others by disease and other misfortunes. It is in this way that much *Karma* from past lives can be worked out. Much heavy *karma* will come into effect in a milder form through the grace of the *Guru*. For example, a *karma* that according to the cosmic law would have caused serious injury can be resolved with a small cut on the finger.

The Master demonstrates great faith in the disciples to whom he shows the *kriya* technique. Nowadays it is not easy to find disciples who take their spiritual path sincerely enough to allow the Master to trust them fully. Unfortunately, with most disciples, their mind changes as fast as the weather.

I hold many seeds in my hands. Wherever I go I will sow these seeds. Some seeds will fall on rock and the birds will eat them, while others will dry out quickly. Only a few of them will sprout and continue to grow.

I give everything I have in the hope that the seeds of my words will now and then fall on fertile ground and grow into a lovely flower or a strong tree.

Kundalini

SHIVA symbolizes consciousness or the male principle. SHAKTI is the female principle or energy. Wherever a force is active and energy is present, *Shakti* is working.

Another name for these two primeval principles is PURUSHA and PRAKRITI. PURUSHA means consciousness, and PRAKRITI means nature.

Only when these two principles are working together can action, movement and creation arise. Energy on its own cannot create. Only consciousness can give it direction and form. Consciousness without *Shakti* is a dormant power. *Shakti* is latent energy, and for this reason is not able to generate any process by itself.

When we are sleeping, our energy is present but we are not conscious of it. As we wake up, consciousness and energy reconnect again. Now we can get up and do something.

For energy to be effective it has to unite with consciousness.

Often the meaning of *Shiva* and *Shakti* are misunderstood. Many see *Shiva* as a man and *Shakti* as a woman, and misinterpret the union of both as a sexual union. This misunderstanding is expressed in a number of nonsensical redemption theories and practices.

Sexuality is completely natural. Each living creature is aware of it without having to learn about it. If humans believe they need to learn about it, they consider their abilities to be less than those of animals. The misunderstanding starts when sexuality and spirituality are confused.

Sexuality is the union of man and woman.

Spirituality is the union of the human and the Divine consciousness.

Kundalini is also a form of *Shakti* ell.

KUND is a deep container or well in which all dirt and rubbish is thrown. With time, the bits of rubbish lose their original form, so you are no longer able to recognise them. They have broken down into a formless pulp. Similarly, all impressions in this and former lives lie deep in the Muladhara *Chakra* in an amorphous form.

KUNDAL means ring (often earring). A ring has no beginning or end. Just like a zero, it starts nowhere and ends nowhere. Other symbols do have an endpoint, but the zero is endless. For this reason, zero symbolizes the universe; cosmic energy circles continually. We do not know when it started, or for how long it will continue.

The letter "i" at the end of the word indicates that *kundalini* is feminine, which means *kundalini* is an expression of the energy of *Prakriti* (nature). In literature it is often referred to as "serpent power".

KAL means snake, or time. What is the connection between these two terms? Time means change or continuation, and the snake symbolizes poison and death. Poison can kill, but can also save lives when used as medicine. Death results in a change of consciousness. Often, the snake is connected to original sin. In Christianity, sin is represented by the symbol of a snake.

In relation to Yoga, the term *kundalini* generally refers to our hidden, sleeping energy.

If you don't know the species of a particular sleeping snake it is better not to touch it, because it might wake up and attack so suddenly you can't escape its bite. Similarly, one should not take medicine if you do not know which dosage is healing or damaging. This means that until you feel you are able to handle the problems that lie deep within you, or work with them once they rise into your consciousness, it is best to let them lie.

In the human body there are 72,000 *nadis* (energy channels) that are spread like a network throughout the entire body. Consciousness (which is energy) flows through these *nadis*.

With the *pranayama* practice of *Nadi Shodhana,* the functions of all *nadis* are awakened. If all 72,000 *nadis* function properly, then the person is healthy. Nearly everyone has some type of problem with their health, which means some of the *nadis* are not working properly.

The *nadis* are channels through which the cosmic energy – *prana* or vitality – is taken in and distributed throughout the whole body. *Prana* is the source of all life and the *nadis* are the pathways for this energy within us.

Prana is conscious energy, and therefore the *Nadis* transport consciousness. With the help of the *nadis,* one can see and hear things far away, as well as experiencing other planes of consciousness. There are numerous reports where people who have had near death experiences and are then brought back to life describe tunnels through which they wandered and a light they often saw at the end of them. These tunnels are the *nadis*.

The central station of consciousness is the brain, but when the *Atma* does finally leave the body, this central station breaks down. At this point, we will not be able to see any more tunnels. When astral travelling, we can have visions of tunnels or see the body from the outside. In reality, we are merely in an altered state of consciousness and not actually outside the body. We can travel millions of kilometres without actually leaving the body for a single moment. When we dream of India, for example, we only experience this faraway journey at the level of consciousness. The *nadis* allow us mental journeys of discovery throughout the whole universe.

There are two *nadis*, which are of special significance: *Ida* and *Pingala*. These two *nadis* maintain the balance between *Shiva* (consciousness) and *Shakti* (energy).

In this case, *Shakti* means emotion. Emotion means "in motion". When the sleeping energy awakens, a movement begins to set in motion all life functions. Emotions, feelings and the connected thoughts never stay the same; they are constantly changing.

Don't allow yourself to be dependent on your moods, otherwise you will never be happy and content.

Feelings and emotions are connected with the lunar principle. Like the moon, feelings also continuously change shape. The power of the moon moves even the huge oceans by creating the tides. The moon influences all of nature, as well as our consciousness. Many people cannot sleep on a full moon night. Others suffer from depression or migraines. Many animals and people respond with nervousness or aggression.

Both male and female forces exist in all of us. In many depictions of Lord Shiva these two primordial powers are symbolized in each half of the body; the left side is the feminine (*Parvati*) and the right side is the masculine (*Shiva*).

Men are drawn to female qualities and woman to masculine. For this reason, the male consciousness is attracted to the female gender and vice versa. If both tendencies are balanced no sexual energy can flow and no sexual attraction is generated. If, however, men are predominantly drawn to male qualities and women are predominantly drawn to female qualities, attraction to the same gender will be the result.

The functioning of the *nadis* and the flow of *prana* influence both feelings and consciousness because *prana*, life force, influences everything. Through the practice of *pranayama*, breathing exercises, the male and female energies within us can be harmonized. *Pranayama* is the science of the function and control of *prana*.

IDA symbolizes the moon and originates on the left side of the body. *PINGALA* symbolizes the sun and starts on the right side of the body. In order to maintain balance, *Ida* influences the right side and *Pingala* the left. Through medical science we know that the right half of the brain coordinates the left side of the body, and the left half of the brain coordinates the right side. The Yogis already recognised these functions many thousands of years ago.

Because the right energy channel influences the left side of the body, and the left energy channel influences the right side, there has to be a point where the energy of the two *Nadis* meets and flows together. The coming together of these two *nadis* occurs in the central *nadi*, *Sushumna*.

Ida and *Pingala* cross *Sushumna*, the central channel, several times, because each of them is continually attracted to its polar opposite. The points where all three *nadis* meet are called *chakras*. Energy centres are formed at these very energy-rich locations. At the end of the spine, at the *Root Chakra*, or *Muladhara Chakra*, the left *nadi* finally returns to the left side of the body, and the right *nadi* to the right side. At this point the movement stops. It is precisely at this point that our sleeping consciousness lies hidden. The path of the two *nadis* follows hairpin bends and curves that resemble the movements of a snake. That is why these streams of energy are also called "serpent power". Fortunately, a real snake is not wandering up our spine!

The *kundalini* is symbolically shown as a curled up, or sleeping snake, coiled three and a half times with its head pointing upwards. This symbolizes the three levels of consciousness – the unconscious, subconscious and conscious. The half coil pointing downwards indicates that the awakened part of the human consciousness can sink back down into lower planes through pride and negatively-focused intellect. Humans arrogantly think of themselves as the most highly developed beings, but they are currently in the process of destroying the whole world.

For humans, the path to realisation and right understanding is hard, because they have to allow their ego to dissolve. Jesus gave us a great example of this when he washed and oiled the feet of his disciples. People only want to surrender to God and not to any other living being. But our vanity, pride and egotistical focus on ourselves make us blind to the truth that God lives in all.

With the washing of his disciples' feet, Jesus also demonstrated that we need to help others in the purification of their *karmas*, and in overcoming their lower traits. We need to support them in the purification of body, mind and consciousness.

Do good for yourself and others – that is Yoga in Daily Life®!

A wise and Self-realised person is always humble. Wisdom does not come unbidden. All thoughts must be purified and all actions directed to the positive. Those people who do not serve other living beings and cannot surrender to anything, do not know God. They are filled with fear and complexes.

A great Saint said,

> "God is in every heart; no heart is empty. I devote my life to the people in whose heart God has begun to speak."

What does the awakening of *kundalini* mean? It means the awakening of wisdom and knowledge. When knowledge is there, clarity will arise.

If something falls out of your hand and breaks on the floor, you are angry. You can only direct this anger to yourself because you have been inattentive. Whoever is conscious of holding something in their hand will definitely not drop it.

An enlightened person is completely conscious when their *kundalini* is awakened. The energy of this consciousness is so strong it is difficult for the body to withstand it. It is as if you screw a light bulb into 5000 watts instead of 100 watts. In order to be able to handle this enormous spiritual energy, the body and the *nadis* have to be prepared and purified in the proper way.

Awakening of the *kundalini* means pure joy. You are free and nothing holds you back anymore. You radiate such all-encompassing love that everyone feels attracted to you.

Awakening of the *kundalini* is the awakening of consciousness.

I will give you an example of this process:

Assume you have lost your car keys and don't know where they are. This indicates that the keys no longer exist in your consciousness. Eventually somebody tells you where they are, and as soon as you rediscover the keys they appear again in your consciousness. Not knowing has changed into certainty. Ignorance has disappeared and knowledge has taken its place.

The five lower *chakras* are related to the development of human consciousness after overcoming any animal qualities within them. They are also responsible for the five elements within the body: *Muladhara* for earth; *Svadhishthana* for water; *Manipura* for fire; *Anahata* for air; and *Vishuddhi* for space. The three higher *Chakras – Agya, Bindu* and *Sahasrara* – possess pure human and divine qualities. Those whose *Sahasrara Chakra* is awakened will enter into the Divine light of cosmic consciousness.

Yoga is the science of consciousness and energy.

When *Prakriti* and *Purusha* unite in the *Sahasrara Chakra,* knowledge, knower and object dissolve and become one. In this state of absolute consciousness, no polarity exists and therefore neither does suffering; only joy, love, tolerance and understanding for all living beings. While we are still connected with the physical body, consciousness will again return from the *Sahasrara* and reside in the *Anahata*, the Heart Centre. The heart becomes the divine residence. A realised person always acts only from the heart. That person lives in eternal love and happiness, is conscious of the internal immortal soul – the ocean of bliss – and will forever lead a divine live.

To reach this state of certainty, the Yogi is prepared to give up everything of this world and to renounce all. In him resounds the song that was sung by Paramhans Yogananda:

"Door of my heart, open wide I keep for Thee.
Wilt Thou come, wilt Thou come!
Just for once, come to me.
I look for Thee night and day!"

There are two categories of people who can't sleep.

Firstly, the Yogi who cannot sleep because he is waiting for God day and night, longing for Divine love. Secondly, the sick person whose pain is robbing him of sleep. The ignorant, however, sleep deeply and for a long time – thousands of life times.

In the following *bhajan* a seeker is lamenting to God:

"Oh, you cruel one! At least come to me once in my
dreams to soothe my pains.
Had I only known that a glimpse of your eyes would
awaken such pain of longing in me...!
Oh, you insensitive one! At least come to me once in my
dreams to soothe my pains.
I have renounced everything for this one glimpse.
When I tell you of my feelings, you get annoyed with me.
Not to reveal my feelings however would burn up my
heart!"

That is the state of a seeker who is in love with God. He searches day and night – and one day God will definitely come to such a pure heart!

Dive into your inner Self and pray to the divine *Shakti,* who lives in every cell of your body. Without this *shakti,* we could not exist for even one moment. *Shakti* is the divine mother: she protects, nurtures and loves us.

On the other hand, our consciousness represents the fatherly love of God.

When we are aware of this, we know that we possess everything within us. Due to our good fortune and good *karma* from past lives, we have received a human body. Thanks to God's grace we have been led to the spiritual path and brought into contact with Yoga.

I wish for you the blessings of the divine mother who manifests in you as life force and vitality. May she always protect and nurture you. May the divine father and mother lead you in their perfect love to cosmic consciousness.

I pray to Mahaprabhuji for protection, divine guidance and enlightenment for all of you.

May God bless you all!

DOOR OF MY HEART

Door of my heart
Open wide I keep for Thee
Wilt Thou come wilt Thou come
Just for once come to me.

Will my days fly away
Without seeing Thee my Lord
Night and day night and day
I look for Thee night and day

Paramhans Yogananda

Satsang

SATSANG is of extraordinary importance on the spiritual path.

SAT is the truth, while SANG means company.

In *satsang* we talk about God.

Satsang is the best way to develop *viveka* and to overcome all problems in life. In *satsang,* your *karmas* are purified.

Satsang is the ferry of Mahaprabhuji. He will bring you safely to the other shore – but, of course, only if you stay in the boat. For those who jump out, it is not certain if they will ever reach the other shore. For this reason, I ask you to keep going, whether you feel comfortable in this ferry or not.

Those who feel happy and content within are the ones who are particularly blessed. For those who allow their love for Mahaprabhuji to flow whole-heartedly, nothing else will stick. In this way, bliss and wisdom become anchored in their hearts.

This goal cannot be achieved merely through certain practices and disciplines, as they cannot remove the roots of discontent buried deep in your unconscious.

Pray to God, and He will help you. We can only be grateful for His protection. After much suffering, you have finally been born as a human and have met your Master. Finally, you have achieved this. Now you live in the Light, in the light of the wisdom of Yoga, in the light of Sri Deep Narayan Mahaprabhuji. Be aware of your good fortune in having arrived at the point of being able to live a spiritual life. Use this life to do good for all people.

I don't expect anything from you. I am only here to give you what I know. I am a river that flows, and you have come to its shore. You can clean yourself in this river, you can swim in it, you can drink from it, or you can leave it thirsty. It all depends on you.

Even if you reject it, the river will continue to flow. You can throw stones in the river and it will not ask you why you have done this.

Wisdom flows in this river.

I hope and pray that we will have many more *satsangs* together. But no one knows how much longer our body will accompany us on this journey.

My words not only accompany you in this physical world, but also on the astral plane.

Try and take something from each *satsang* for your own personal development. Pay attention, understand, realise and purify; purify everything. Bring your intellect and emotions into harmony and unite them.

Satsangs will assist you greatly in achieving this.

Why we sing Bhajans

There are four ages, or YUGAS: SATYA YUGA, TRETA YUGA, DVAPA-RA YUGA and KALI YUGA.

SATYA YUGA is the age of GYANA YOGA, the path of knowledge. Knowledge creates clarity, balance and perfection.

TRETA YUGA is the age of RAJA YOGA, the "kingly" path of Yoga. Discipline and creativity are the fundamental principles.

DVAPARA YUGA is the age of KARMA YOGA, of selfless service, in which work, helping and the fulfilment of DHARMA open the way to union.

KALI YUGA, the "dark age" and our present, is the time in which only BHAKTI, or selfless love and devotion, can lead us to liberation. Deep knowledge, strong discipline and creative energy are not characteristic of people in our time. It is most important for the attainment of our life's goal to both show and give love.

Narada, a great Saint, once asked Lord Vishnu, "Lord, where do you mostly reside? In *Vaikuntha* (the heaven), or in the hearts of Yogis who meditate on you?" Lord Vishnu replied, "Mostly I am found neither in the heaven of the Gods, nor in the hearts of meditators, but rather where my *Bhaktas*, my devotees, sing my name with love."

In *Kali Yuga,* the best way to awaken *bhakti* is by singing *bhajan*s.

Sri Devpuriji said: "Each action that is done in the name of *Gurudev* is successful. There is no power in the universe that can stop a devotee of God, because God himself will take on the *karmas* of the devotee."

Try to be true children of God; surrender to Him and trust His guidance.

In *Kali Yuga,* the SADHANA (practice) that is most likely to succeed is the path of BHAKTI YOGA. The singing of *bhajan*s is a part of *Bhakti Yoga.* Singing is an inspiration; it awakens our feelings and consciousness, and brings wisdom and clarity. It strengthens our inner willpower to continue on the path, helping us to overcome problems and difficulties. It is the language of the heart. The vibration of the sound touches our innermost core, even when we don't understand the language of the song.

Spiritual songs are GURU VAKYA, or words of the *Guru.* They are the words of God-realised people. Divine love inspires such great souls to compose *bhajan*s, which have such a pure and clear vibration that they continue to resound in the soul. A song that comes from deep love and devotion touches the hearts of all people, whatever religion or culture they belong to, because Love is God and God is Love.

If, however, someone sings without devotion, with only superficial feelings, the result will be different:

A group of musicians and singers were very proud of their supposedly unsurpassed art of playing ragas.

The word *raga* has two meanings. On one hand it means melody, but on the other it means attachment.

They announced they would play a concert in one village. Many people came, all very curious to hear their performance. But after a short while, almost half the people left the concert. After barely an hour, a quarter of the spectators remained, and finally only one old woman stayed behind.

The musicians thought to themselves: "At least one person understands our music." So, they continued their performance, convinced of their outstanding art. When they saw that the woman had even started to cry, they thought, "This woman really understands art. She is so deeply touched that she is actually crying."

At four o'clock in the morning the old woman was still sitting there crying. Finally, one of the singers approached her and asked, "Mataji, why are you crying?"

The woman answered, sobbing, "I am crying because I feel so sorry for you all. I had a few sheep and goats, which suddenly all fell ill. They cried and howled the whole night and, in the morning, when the sun came up, they were all dead. It sounded just like your singing and that is why I believe that you will all die soon."

Deeply perplexed, the musicians packed their instruments and quickly snuck away quietly and secretly.

Singing does not just mean to produce a melody. It is more important to allow the vibration of your inner love to flow through into every sound.

The *dharma* of each human being is to protect, help, forgive and love all, and also to recognise and realise God. To achieve this, everyone needs to utilise all their power and concentration. Once your time on this earth has expired, it is irrevocably over. What happens to you after that is determined wholly by your *karmas*.

The singing of *bhajan*s is a part of *Bhakti Yoga*. *Bhakti* is the primary path in *Kali Yuga*, because in *Kali Yuga* God takes on the *karmas* of His *bhaktas* and protects them from all adversities. For this reason, develop your love, devotion and trust in God rather than wasting your time with unimportant, impermanent things.

Trust

To be born into this world is like jumping into a torrential river, filled with crocodiles. Our desires and qualities are like the crocodiles. Sometimes, we even fall into the water without being able to swim – and that is truly dangerous.

Each one of us has to battle with difficulties during our lifetime. We make our own mistakes and are affected by the mistakes of others. When walking through a coal mine, one can easily end up with black spots. As humans, we wander through the coal mine of our ignorance.

Often, we cannot clearly distinguish between imagination and reality, and our perception of things does not coincide with the actual facts. Even though we may act with the best intentions, the outcome may differ from what we had expected it to be.

Only God can free us from the ocean of MAYA, and for this reason, you must put all your trust in Him.

But often we lack trust.

> A farmer's boy had the duty of taking the cows and goats to the pasture after school and looking after them.

Such relatively easy but responsible tasks are well suited for children. In this way, they can learn to consciously take care of something. The ability to care and a sense of duty are the basis of a mature personality.

Once the boy tied a rope around the neck of a very thirsty goat and led her to the water. When they reached the water, the boy guided her to the spot on the shore where it would be the easiest for her to drink. Suddenly, the goat became stubborn and started to resist him. With all her might she used her front legs to push against his well-intentioned guidance and refused to take another single step forward. Even though she was really thirsty and saw the water so close to her, her obstinacy was stronger than her reason.

Many disciples react in a similar way due to countless complexes that exist in their subconscious, which create obstacles to their progress.

In India we say, *"People who are happy and content have so much love inside them because they were able to spend a long period of time with God before they came back to Earth."* They were not in as much of a hurry to jump back into this world. I believe I was also allowed to spend a long time with God before I came back to earth in possession of His blessings and a big task.

You put your life into my hands with full confidence. It is like a piece of clay in the hands of a Master who knows how to create an artistic masterpiece. Never take my directions as orders, but instead receive them with full trust as guidance for your spiritual development.

All of us have a very special, deep bond with each other, and a *karmic* connection. Many thousands of people who are not yet spiritually awakened, or even born, are still coming to join us. Our relationship is not a physical or social one. It is a spiritual and divine connection. The basis of this connection is total trust, which will guide us all and finally bring all of you to your goal.

Do not miss your chance!

No one is asking you to completely change your life. Live in the way you have been living to date – but from now on live CONSCIOUSLY!

Sometimes we believe we are doing the right thing, but later on it proves to be a mistake. Once you have made a mistake, the most important thing is not to get stuck in it. If you have fallen, get up and keep walking. Then you will be helped!

Everyone makes mistakes. Just don't keep repeating the same mistakes. Wake up and live consciously!

Holy Guruji says in a *bhajan*:

> *BHAI TUMA JAGO RE*
> *Brothers wake up! Wake up! Otherwise*
> *you will miss your chance.*

The chance to be born as a human is very rare and precious.

> *A Master lived a peaceful and harmonious life in his Ashram together with his disciple. One day the disciple said, "Master, I would like to go into town."*
> *The Master asked, "Why? What do you want to do in town?"*
> *The disciple replied, "In town I can meet friends and go out with them. Here I feel so lonely and isolated from everything. Please, Master, allow me to go to town."*
> *The Master objected. "You have duties to fulfil. You need to milk the cows, and take care of the altar and the ashram."*

The disciple begged further, "I would like to go into town so much!"

Seemingly, the Master gave in. "Okay, you can go, but please wait a few more days, until I have found someone who can take over your duties."

In the night, the Master meditated on the reason why his disciple wanted to go to town so much. Each desire that arises in our consciousness has its cause. The Master found out that the karma of his disciple had to do with a certain food that was available in town from a certain family. Because he now knew the cause for his disciple's sudden discontentment, he asked someone to go to this family in town and to bring the food back with them.

Then he called his disciple and said: "Before going to town, have a few days' rest and then you may go." During this time, the Master gave him the food to eat that had been brought from town.

And the thoughts of the disciple started to change in a marvellous way. He began to ask himself, "Why should I go to town? Where will I stay, where will I sleep? In town I am only a stranger, and here I am at home. I enjoy nature and the blessing of the Satsang and darshan of my Master."

After a few days he decided for himself, "I won't go to town! I would be a fool to exchange satsang for kusang."

Just at this moment, the Master called the disciple and said, "I have found someone who will take care of the ashram. Now you can make your way into town."

The disciple replied, "Master I don't wish to go anymore."

"But you can go," said the Master.

"But I don't want to anymore," the disciple insisted.

"Tell me why?" the Master wanted to know.

The disciple named several reasons; whatever came into his mind. Only the Master, however, knew the truth.

There are always occasions that entice you off the spiritual path. But only rarely will you know the true reason behind it.

In India we have a saying: "On each grain of corn is written the name of the person whose food it is meant to be."

Whether for a person or an animal, each grain is destined for a specific living being, and no one else will receive it. I will tell you a story relating to this:

A Yogi once passed by a house. A woman sat outside the house washing rice. The Yogi gave her a thoughtful smile and asked, "For whom are you washing this rice?"
The woman answered, "For my family to have for dinner. But why are you smiling about this?"
The Yogi explained, "I am having a laugh about destiny. Within this rice that you are washing, is one grain that is destined for the King."
The woman laughed and said, "Well the king is certainly not coming here for dinner!"
In the evening the husband brought a guest, who was the treasurer of a rich merchant, to dinner. The following day the merchant was called to the king. Together with his treasurer they went to the palace.
During their business negotiations, the treasurer had to sneeze several times. A grain of rice, which had been stuck between his teeth from the night before, flew out of his mouth and landed on the king's robe. To the treasurer's great relief, nobody noticed anything. During the conversation the king, while lost in thought, picked it up and put it in his mouth.
When the treasurer returned home he reported to his wife, "Today God really protected me! Yesterday I was invited for dinner and we had rice. A grain of rice got stuck in my teeth and at the palace today when I sneezed, the

grain of rice flew out of my mouth and landed in the King's lap. But fortunately, he did not notice and in his absent-mindedness put it in his mouth."

His wife told the story to others and eventually the woman who had been hostess to the treasurer that night heard of it. Impressed, she commented, "This was predicted by the Yogi. The name of the one for whom it is destined is written on each grain."

Another interesting event happened to me personally:

One person who travelled to India came to visit me, and brought a souvenir from Vienna with them. I kept it and took it back to Vienna. There I gave it to an Indian, who took it back to India and gave it to his mother. When I next travelled to India I visited that family. The mother told me that her son had given her something really beautiful from Vienna and she wanted to give it to me as a present... Well, this present followed me, or I followed it.

We don't know what is destined for whom, so all we can do is trust that what is ours will come to us in time.

Please take my words seriously. Do something with your life and don't waste your time.

GURU VAKYA, the words of the *Guru,* do not just reach you, but also many beings on the astral plane, who are also present here now. The *Guru vakya* of Sri Devpuriji, Mahaprabuji and Holy Guruji resonates through me. Through their strong vibration, your phenomenon is liberated and enlightened. Thank God for every hour that you are able to spend in *satsang. Satsang* is God's blessing. Nothing is more precious than *satsang.*

Mahaprabhuji says in one *bhajan*:

GURUDEVA DARSANA DHANA HO
What a blessing to see Gurudeva!
Through the presence of your Gurudeva,
Your consciousness is filled with ananda (joy).

And Holy Guruji wrote this song:

SRI DIPA DAYALA ARAJA SUNO LIJO
Merciful Mahaprabhuji, please hear my prayer and lead
me to satsang.

Satsang is something Divine. May our ears only hear divine words, and may our legs carry us always to *satsang*. The purpose of this human life is to attain Self-realisation and to serve *Gurudeva*. We should not miss the chance in this life.

For this reason, Holy Guruji reminds us:

BHAI TUMA JAGO RE
Brother, wake up!
You are missing your chance, the chance of human life.
Every minute is precious and irretrievable.
Wake up brother, wake up!

NINDA AVIDYA CHAYA RAHI
TUM JANAMA-JANAMA DUKHA PAYA
You sleep the sleep of ignorance;
for that you will have to suffer many lifetimes.

Why? Because you have not utilised the rare opportunity given by a human life. In life there are many opportunities, but a human birth is very rare. One day, your life on earth will end and what will happen then? If you have not used

119

this opportunity you will have to go through many different existences and experience much suffering.

LAKH CORASI ME JAVOLA
TERE GURU BINA KON SAHAYA
You will again fall back into the wheel of rebirth.
Who will protect you if you are without your Guru?

There are 8.4 million kinds of living beings on this earth. You have parents in every lifetime; but only a human can have a *Guru* and attain God-realisation. Without *mantra* and *Guru kripa*, the grace of the *Guru,* life is not complete.

SATAGURU SARANA SIDHANA PYARE
TERA JANAM SAPHALA HO JAYA
Go to the Satguru, the Master who will lead
you to reality.
Then your life will be successful.

He will show you the truth, even though that might not feel comfortable for you. Go to the *Satguru,* and then your life will be full of harmony, contentment, freedom and purity, and without anxiety. If you follow the words of the *Gurudeva,* you will be liberated in this lifetime and reach the cosmic Light.

MOHA JALA KI PHASI ME
KYU MAKRI JU MAR JAYA
Otherwise you will die in the net of your attachments,
Like a spider that becomes entangled in its own web,
and dies a pitiful death.

Don't live in ignorance. Don't run blindly after your desires. It is high time to recognise what it means to be a human. A missed opportunity will not return. After this life there is either *MOKSHA* (liberation) or suffering for many hundreds of years.

Yoga and the *Guru* can turn your destiny towards the Light.

> MANUSA JANAMA AMOLAKA HIRO
> BAR-BARA NAHI PAYA
> *Human life is an indescribably precious diamond,*
> *which you can't buy.*

Even if you offer God millions of dollars in exchange for five extra years of your life, He will answer you, "*I will not even give you five extra seconds.*" With money you can buy neither life nor God. Your life will last exactly as long as predestined. It is up to you whether you use it or lose it. You will not receive this treasure again so easily.

> MANUSA TANA SE ATMA HIRO
> RAMA MILE GHATA MAYA
> *For this reason, it is best to achieve*
> *Self-realisation in this lifetime.*
> *Only humans can recognise God in their hearts.*

Only the human being can experience what *ATMA* is. The God that you have been looking for on the outside can only be found inside.

> SRI PUJYA BHAGAVAN DIP NARAYAN
> DIN HANSA CETAYA
> *For this reason, I worship Bhagwan Sri Deep*
> *Narayan Mahaprabhuji.*
> *He has awakened the sleeping swan within me –*
> *the Atma and the soul.*

Why have we come together here? Because you have been awakened already. Your love and devotion, your inspiration and connection to Yoga have been developed through *Guru kripa* and *Guru vakya*, and awakened the sleeping consciousness.

> MADHAVANANDA YO GAVATA HE
> SABHI SUNO CITTA LAYA
> *Holy Guruji says:*
> *My beloved, listen attentively to this bhajan*
> *I hope that you will all awaken through it.*

Blessed and fortunate are you because you have come to *satsang*. Practice and become realised – do not waste this opportunity!

Introductory talk for the Intensive Seminar

In the two weeks of the Intensive Seminar, each of you has the opportunity to devote yourself completely to your practice without any distractions from family or professional problems. Many of you receive such a precious opportunity only once a year. Be grateful that it has been given to you and use it well.

The practices that we are going to do in this seminar are called ANUSTHANA. Usually it takes twelve years to do *anusthana*. Whoever devotes themselves exclusively to their spiritual practice for twelve years will have a radiation that shines like pure gold.

Since it is not possible for any of us to practice our *sadhana* for twenty-four hours a day for the next twelve years, we should at least make use of the opportunity to spend twelve days of the year completely devoted to our practice.

Anusthana means to have a specific goal, and in order to reach this goal perform certain practices. During the practice, the practitioner's time, energy, concentration and prayers are dedicated wholly to God.

The goal of our practices is the recognition of the Divine Self within us.

We follow the path of BRAHMA UPASAD, which means that we meditate on the omnipresent God and the all-pervading power of SHIVA.

Lord Krishna said, *"Everyone will realise exactly that which they concentrate on."*

The power of concentrated thought is so mighty that with this power, objects can be materialised and situations manifested. The mastery of this skill is called a TANTRA SIDDHI. In Europe the term TANTRA is often misunderstood. *Tan* means to stretch, while *tra* means to liberate. *Tantra* thus means to expand your energy and your consciousness as far as possible.

Tantra is the science of the elements. It is possible to gain control over the elements through the development of SHANKALPA SHAKTI, the power of wishes. The one who has realised this SIDDHI will have every wish fulfilled. But in your own interest, it is advisable to use this skill with care and responsibility. Only apply it with totally pure thoughts, words and deeds.

Always remember that you cannot hide anything from God. If this knowledge accompanies all your actions then everything you do will turn out well.

> *A disciple came to a Master with the request for a mantra. The Master said, "Before I give you mantra you have to fulfil a task. Here, take this dove and kill it without anybody seeing you."*
> *The disciple went to another room with the dove in his hand, closed all doors and windows and shortly after returned to the Master, saying, "I cannot kill this dove, because you made it a condition that nobody was to watch, however I can see my actions."*
> *The Master replied, "That can easily be changed. Simply close your eyes."*

The disciple went away again but returned quickly and said, "Master, the dove herself is looking at me!"
The Master again replied, "Well simply cover her eyes."
The disciple did just that and took the knife to thrust it into the animal.
And again, he stopped and was unable to kill the dove.
Sadly, because he could not fulfil his task he went to the Master, admitting: "Master I am sorry. I do not know a way to kill this dove without anyone seeing it. You yourself said recently in Satsang that God sees everything".
Joyfully the Master embraced his disciple, "You have passed the test and will receive your mantra today."

All practices and techniques have their own principles. It is only when you follow them with precision that they will have the desired result. The reason why you have not yet reached Self-realisation is simply that none of you have followed all the principles of Yoga in Daily Life® a hundred percent.

Thousands of grains sit in a grain mill and all will be crushed between the millstones. Only a few grains will stay whole. Those grains which stay close to the axle of the mill cannot be reached by the stones. In this way, we all exist between the millstones of our destiny and Maya. Only those who follow the words of the Master will be spared.

The first goal of Yoga in Daily Life® is health in all areas of human existence – physical, mental, social and spiritual.

PHYSICAL HEALTH is of fundamental importance to our existence. The physical body is the essential medium for our work. In order to be able to fulfil our daily duties to the best of our ability, it is important to feel physically well.

The cheapest and most effective medicine to preserve your health is the practice of Yoga. For this, you only discipline, and to dedicate some time to yourself daily.

MENTAL HEALTH means to purify the mind from all negative thoughts and feelings that poison our environment and us, and to develop the qualities of compassion, understanding, forgiveness, love and devotion instead.

SOCIAL HEALTH means to live in an integrated manner within society, to respect its customs and laws, and to support society with selfless work. Social health expresses itself in the willingness to live for others, and to help, support and protect other people. What purpose would this life have if you used it only to look after your own self?

This life was not given to us purely for ourselves, but primarily to help our fellow men. Our life is only successful if we can do good for everyone; for all living beings and for the whole world.

It is not necessary to count what selfless deeds we have done each day, or how many living beings we have helped. However, after some time we may have collected a good deal of positive *karmas* through our efforts and good deeds. This is how it is when we work together for Yoga in Daily Life®. We are already able to harvest some beautiful fruits after twenty years of continuous effort.

Everything takes time. If we want to harvest good fruits, we must first plant good seeds. To put a seed into the ground takes little time, but it does take a lot of time for a strong plant to develop from it. Do not constantly think about how long it will take until you can harvest the fruits. Instead, put all your loving attention into caring for the plant. When the time is ripe, the fruits fall into your lap of their own accord.

Continue with your work, regardless of whatever obstacles you bump into. Obstacles are only there to be overcome.

SPIRITUAL HEALTH also needs to be looked after. The disease that can affect your spiritual life may be even more dangerous and infectious than any disease that affects the physical body. Spiritual disease is caused by fanaticism, intolerance, and a lack of love.

The four aspects of health mentioned here – physical, mental, social and spiritual health – are a means to an end. They are paths to the one goal: achieving Self-realisation and the realisation of God.

Many people, however, who attempt to attain God-realisation have no idea who God really is. To truly recognise and realise God is not easy. It is possible that God is something completely different to what we imagine. Theoretical contemplation is useless. Reality needs to be lived and experienced.

Wherever *prana* exists, movement is the result. Where you find movement, a process or development takes place.

Without *prana,* movement is impossible. Lord Krishna said to Arjuna, *"Without my Will, not even a single leaf on a tree can move."*

How can we understand this? What is the Will of God? Does God even have a Will?

The Will of God is not comparable with our human will, as we would usually imagine. The Will of God is more like a principle, an element or *prana*. It is also called ISHVARA. Ishvara is the formless, all-pervading and omnipresent aspect of God. God's *Shakti* (energy) penetrates everything and is present everywhere, whether it appears to be "good" or "bad". Energy by itself is neutral and is called good or bad by us depending on how it is used.

Follow these four principles in each *anusthana*:

1. EAT LITTLE.
   Mahaprabhuji said, "Two things are very difficult for people: To forgive and to eat little."
   Who eats less, has more energy. We can also lose energy through eating too much. Everyone knows how tired you can feel after a big meal.

2. *MAUNA* – SILENCE
   Each spoken word means a loss of energy. It is better to use your time and energy for your Sadhana.
   In western society they say, "Time is money".
   In India, however, they know, "Time is so precious, you cannot pay for it with money."

3. AVOID PHYSICAL CONTACT
   Even touching another person can dissipate your energy.

4. PURITY
   By purity, we mean both physical and mental purity. To stay mentally pure means not to allow any impure thoughts into your mind.

This is the state of VAIRAGYA. Whoever has experienced this state knows of the wonderful freedom that you feel.

Think of God in every activity. Go to sleep thinking of God and get up in the morning thinking of God as well. Dedicate your whole practice to God.

When you are thinking of God it is impossible for impure thoughts to enter your phenomenon.

A few years ago, I met an old man who was sitting on a park bench looking sad and lonely. I sensed his longing to be able to speak to someone, and sat beside him.
He said, "Why do I have to live for such a long time? All my friends have died already. I have worked very hard all my life to provide for my family. My wife is dead and two of my children have also died. I only have one daughter left, but she lives in Germany and only calls me every now and then. I am now completely on my own living in a nursing home. Often, I ask myself, 'What is the purpose of such a life?'"

You are also growing older every day. Try to recognise the true purpose of life now, otherwise one day you will feel very, very sorry. For anyone who entrusts his life unto God, each day is a golden day. For everyone else, the whole of life exists only in the painful roller coaster of happiness and misery.

Think about whether you have wasted your time, or whether hour-by-hour you are gaining something for your development.

Do not let the fate of the old man be what happens to you. Make sure that one day you will not be saying, "Now it is too late!"

I pray to Mahaprabhuji that He may give you Light, bliss and a beautiful, spiritual experience in your *anusthana*.

Disturbances on your Path

In the universe three TAPAS (disturbances) are at work: *ADHI-BHAUTIKA, ADHI-DAIVIKA* and *ADHI-ATMIKA*.

ADHI-BHAUTIKA are external disturbances, created by physical causes or other living beings.
ADHI-DAIVIKA are disturbances that come from invisible astral forces or beings.
ADHI-ATMIKA are disturbances from the level of the *Tattvas* (elements), which exist beyond the material and astral worlds.

Whatever happens to you does not occur by accident. It is caused by your *karma* directing your phenomenon into the resultant situation. This will happen until you have finally attained liberation from the wheel of birth and rebirth after many, many lives. The most important task in life is to purify yourself from your *karmas.*

Nothing on this earthly plane is able to give us pure bliss, because ultimately everything is bound to decay. But truth does not change. Only this reality will give us permanent contentment. Sometimes an accident or a difficult disease will lead us onto the spiritual path. It is then that we realise possessions and relationships will not satisfy us forever. Often such a "tragic" event (tragic in the worldly sense) will make us think about the true purpose of life for the first time.

To give freedom means to have freedom at the same time. While holding a snake in your hand, the snake is not free, but neither are you. Giving the snake its freedom will set you both free.

Most people are bound to several things at the same time. They live in political, social, familial, religious and economic dependence. We build the walls of our prison with our own hands, creating the difficulties against which we will later have to fight.

The cosmic law is above all laws; the natural law is ruled by the cosmic law. Humans have removed themselves far from the natural law, because they only want to recognise their own human laws. Often, unfortunately, human laws are not in harmony with the law of nature, and this is why there are wars, famine, poverty and all the other problems happening in this world.

God is the giver of the cosmic law. All wars would end immediately if all of humanity would follow the words of the holy Vedas:

VISHWA PRANI MERI ATMA HE
All living beings in this universe are my Atma.

ATMA SO PARAMATMA, PARAMATMA SO ATMA
Atma is God, and God is the Atma.

We all are brothers and sisters. Jesus said, *"Love your neighbour!"* Who of us has such love? If we would all have this love, we could create paradise on earth. Unfortunately, humans have not yet stopped fighting for power and possessions.

Be ready to make sacrifices for your spiritual development. Not only material sacrifices, but the sacrifice of your inner feelings such as attachment, jealousy, hate and doubt. Practice selflessness, and work without expecting any fruits from your work. Then you will make great progress on your spiritual path and purify your *karmas*.

Prayer, *Mantra* and sacrifice are the most effective means against all destructive forces. Renounce, sacrifice, give to others, and be selfless. Disturbances happen when selfishness prevails. Sing the GAYATRI MANTRA each morning five times and after that, the peace *Mantra* OM SHANTI three times. These *mantras* form a protective cloak against the three *tapas* – *adhi-bhautika, adhi-daivika* and *adhi-atmika*.

OM BHUR BHUVAH SVAHA TAT SAVITUR VARENYAM
BHARGO DEVASYA DHIMAHI DHIYO YO NA PRACHODAYAT
OM SHANTIH SHANTIH SHANTIH

*Let us meditate on the wondrous and merciful divine
light that is anchored in our hearts.
May it unfold all our potential, may it guide our intellect
and enlighten our understanding.
OM Peace Peace Peace.*

Your Obstacle

The biggest disappointment is when
you disappoint yourself.
The greatest sin is when you lie to yourself.
The biggest mistake is the one you
make towards yourself.
What is this mistake?

The mistake is thinking of things from the external world as important and indispensable, and thus allowing them to make too many demands on you. This is a fallacy and the cause of your decline. By chasing them, you are running towards your own destruction.

You need to consciously protect yourself from this self-destruction. Don't be your own obstacle!

Your desires, feelings and thoughts can form considerable obstacles for you. For this reason, you must follow the words of Divine incarnations like Mahaprabhuji, Krishna or Jesus.

Who was Jesus? He was a Master. What is the Bible? It is a dialogue between a Master and His disciples. The Bhagavad Gita is also a dialogue between a Master and His disciples.

And this *satsang* is a dialogue between you and me.

Some people understand, others don't. Some only understand for a short period and immediately forget it all again as soon as they are confronted with new subjects. The words that you have understood should remain in your memory forever!

Ask yourself what you really want. What is your DHARMA and why have you come here? Tell yourself, *"Let go of all illusion, turn to your own truth!"* And pray to God, *"My Divine Lord, I worship you, I pray to you. Please lead me to Reality!"*

Until you have realised SAM and DAM, you will act as your own obstacle and lead yourself into disappointments again and again. SAM means to hold back the senses and emotions. DAM means the inner watchfulness and control of feelings and desires.

What are those disappointments that you experience through your feelings? You run here and there and can never find what you are looking for.

In the *bhajan* BHAI TUM JAGO RE, Holy Guruji tells us:

MANUSA JANAMA AMOLAKA HIRO
"This precious diamond of human life will not be given to you so easily again."

LAKH CORASI ME JAVOLA
TERE GURU BINA KON SAHAYA
"And again, you will have to go through the cycle of the 8.4 million beings.
Who will protect you then, so far away from your Gurudeva?"

Follow *Guru vakya*; follow the words of *Gurudeva*. Whatever your Master says to you is good and will help your development. Even if sometimes His instructions seem inexplicable, difficult or painful, know they are always in your best interests, and will help you to remove the obstacles on your path.

Fear comes from Ignorance

Ignorance is the root cause of a multitude of problems in our life. Ignorance causes incorrect ideas and misunderstandings from which we often suffer enormously.

Where there is ignorance, there is duality. Knowledge, however, means union with God.

SO HAM – That I am. I am that.

You are not a sinner, and you do not need to be afraid of punishment. Your *Atma* is God. Sin does not exist in the *Atma*, only on the physical and astral plane and in your thoughts. God will never punish you. You are His child and He loves you immensely.

Fear is ignorance. Everyone makes mistakes whilst they are alive. As long as you believe in God's punishment, almost any experience will evoke fear in you. Complexes result in fear. We feel we are sinners and are afraid of God's punishment. The cause of these complexes lies only in our conditioning, which is a result of our education, society and culture.

Try to recognise who you really are.

A person who has realised God will never boast about it in front of others. Most people become jealous if someone has more than them, as no-one wants another person standing above them. This is the reason for all the wars and fighting. That is why God is hiding from us; He is hiding from the arrogant pride of humanity.

Whoever is truly searching for God is not striving for exceptional experiences. Be content and happy wherever you are and whatever you are doing. Do not hurry.

Keep the experiences you have in your meditations and prayers to yourself. Observe, try to understand, and learn from your experiences. Look at how your life was before this experience and how it is different because of it. Do you feel closer to God? Has something changed in your way of thinking?

Whatever experience you have had, the most important thing is to be closer to God and to overcome your *Karmas*. Our experiences will guide and direct us.

Your inner Self is God, and God is your inner Self. He lives within you as Light.

Realisation means non-duality. Duality comes from ignorance and wherever there is ignorance, suffering exists.

Imagine you are going for a walk at night. Suddenly you see something before you on the path that looks like a snake. Fear arises in you. In the torchlight you recognise with great relief that it is only a rope lying on the ground. Smiling about your anxiety, you take the rope and throw it aside.

Where did the fear of the snake come from? Where did the snake go and the fear with it?

The snake appeared because of your ignorance, and this created fear. Upon shining the light of knowledge and recognition, the snake delusion dissolved, and all your fear was instantly blown away. Reality was different to what you thought it was.

Whatever you have learnt, keep it safe in your heart and use it for your further development.

These are the words of Bhagwan Sri Deep Narayan Mahaprabhuji. You can be sure that He will always guide you. He is the Holy Father, and we are His children. Every father loves his children very much.

To be born as a human is a great fortune.

Know that you are not a sinner.

You are *Atma*, pure Consciousness and the Light of God. You are the Light of the universe.

Attachment

Only in the last minutes of our life will we know if we have used our time well in this lifetime. Most of what seems incredibly important today will be completely meaningless to us after death.

Kabirdas, the great Indian poet and philosopher, speaks in a *bhajan* about parrots that allow themselves to be seduced again and again by beautiful fruits.

> *There are some trees in the Indian mountains that carry a fruit that is about the size of a plum. They are very attractive to parrots because of their bright red colour. Therefore, you often see marvellous birds in these trees. But when the parrot tries to open a fruit with his beak, it cracks open and the unpalatable gluey substance it contains winds around his beak making it very sticky. The bird gains nothing from this fruit, and experiences only the anger and effort of having to clean it off again. Still, he cannot resist this enticing looking fruit. Unable to learn, he will open one fruit after the other, his attention again and again attracted by even more beautiful and bigger fruits.*

Kabirdas compares these fruits to *MAYA*, and the birds to humans. Similarly, we keep ourselves busy with many things that are of absolutely no use to us. Instead, we need to always remember that our possessions, however precious they are to us, and our friends and relatives, however much we love them, will not accompany us any further than the hour of our death.

A young man spent the best part of his time with his Master. The parents of the young man did not agree with this, and in order to distract him, they found him a bride. Soon the wedding took place, but satsang with His Master remained the main objective in his life. His parents were very annoyed about this and convinced the daughter-in-law that her marriage was bad because her husband spent most of his time in an Ashram instead of at home. They stirred the jealousy of the young woman until she decided to do something to keep her husband away from his Master.

The next evening when he came home from the Ashram he found his wife crying bitterly. In dismay, he asked her what had happened. Pretending to be hurt, she hypocritically reproached him, "I feel you have no interest in me anymore. Had I known that you would give all your love to your Master I would not have married you. You know I cannot live without you and you should not leave me alone so much."

The man was surprised and also flattered. "She loves me so much that she cannot live without me! Then what my Master says that there is no true love on earth cannot be so." Moved by her words, he promised from now on to stay with his wife always and no longer go to the Ashram. Some weeks passed without him visiting his Master. One day he met his Master in the forest on His daily morning walk. Joyfully he ran towards Him and bowed before Him. "You have not been to the Ashram for a while," remarked the Master.

The disciple replied, "I know Master, but believe me, I do carry you in my heart. But life with my wife is so fulfilling that I can no longer find the time to come and see you."

"I understand, Maya has captured you with her claws!"

"No Master that is not how it is! Finally, I have found true love and that makes me extremely happy," the disciple replied effusively.

"I can prove to you the opposite in no time," the Master assured him. "Follow my instructions precisely. Return home immediately and collapse on the terrace as if fainting. Pretend to your wife that you are suffering from heavy cramping. To be on the safe side hold on tightly to one of the columns with your legs so no one can detach you from it. Then enter the state of Savikalpa Samadhi, in which you can hear and see everything happening around you while appearing dead to everyone else. I promise that you will then realise the true feeling of your family towards you."

The disciple did exactly as the Master suggested. With seemingly heavy cramping, he broke down in front of the house and went into Savikalpa Samadhi. In dismay his wife rushed towards him. Worried, she checked his pulse and his breath, and then thinking that he was dead, she said to herself, "Thank God I finally got rid of him!"

She then proceeded to lament and called the parents of her husband. They all cried loudly for the young man as the custom required. When this was done they tried to carry away his body. They did not succeed because his legs were tightly wrapped around the column. First, they thought of taking down the column, but it could have caused the whole house to fall down. So, they quickly decided to hack off the dead man's legs and his wife hurried to fetch an axe.

With growing horror, the disciple listened and thought anxiously, "Oh Master, what have you done to me? When she comes back with the axe I will not wait any longer and quickly move my legs away!"

Just at this moment the Master appeared and innocently asked what was happening. Crying they told him of the

*tragic death. The Master consoled them, "Do not worry,
I know a secret mantra, that will bring your dear relative
back to life immediately. I need only a bit of milk and
honey."*

*Quickly they brought these to him and carefully the
Master stirred the honey into the milk while murmuring
a mantra. Then he said to the family, "One of you may
now drink this milk. Whoever drinks it will die. The dead,
however, will wake immediately."*

*He turned to the father and said, "Just now I heard you
lamenting about the injustice in the world and how your
son had to die in the flower of his youth, and you, an old
man are still alive. Drink the milk and save your son!"*

*Promptly the old man rejected the idea, "My time has not
yet come to die! I still wish to enjoy my life a bit longer!"*

*Then the Master spoke to the mother: "A mother's love is
the strongest love in the world. With tears you swore that
you would joyfully give your life if you could wake your
son from the dead. Now you can drink the milk."*

*Just as dismayed as the father, the mother rejected the
idea with the excuse that in order to fulfil her marital duty
she could not leave her husband alone in this world.*

*Then finally the Master approached the wife of his disci-
ple and offered her the glass: "Surely you will happily sacrifice yourself for your husband, since you always assured
him that you could not live without him!"*

*But she openly confessed, "No way! I am delighted to
finally be free again!"*

*Then the Master declared that there was nothing left to
do but for him to drink the milk. They all happily agreed
and wordily praised his noble-mindedness.*

*The Master sat down and slowly emptied the glass. Then
he said to his disciple, "Now you can return from your samadhi and freely decide where you wish to go."*

The disciple got up and followed his Master without turning back even once.

Maya leads us to believe many things. She promises us eternal love and ongoing happiness, but after death nobody accompanies us. Only our *karmas*, our wisdom and our spirituality come with us.

Love your fellow human, help wherever you can, but do so without any dependencies or attachments, and never lose sight of your goal.

Freedom

To become the disciple of a spiritual Master means to enter the path to *Moksha*, or liberation.

The first step to freedom is being free of fear. Free of the fear of death, sin, *karma* and dependency. Our life should be free of these.

Every ideology that uses fear as a means to win and keep followers will be a failure in the end. The longing to be free is the nature of human beings. Unfortunately, some denominational and political systems put strong psychic pressure on people. This results in the creation of boundaries, fanaticism and animosity towards members of other belief systems. Without the suppression of a people by those few who hold political and religious power, fighting would soon stop and humans could finally live in happiness and freedom.

To put down other religions and incarnations is, in reality, to revile the same God you are so busy adoring in your own religion. Humans are only harming themselves with their fanaticism and are continuing to spread darkness and suffering in the world.

Mahaprabhuji always attempted to smooth quarrels between the members of different religions. He tried to make it clear to them that misunderstandings are at the root of their fighting. He said:

"Hindus do not know who Krishna and Rama are and the Moslems have forgotten Allah. Had they realised Allah in themselves they would also know Krishna and Rama – and vice versa."

Whatever you do, do it with clear conscience and free will, never be compelled by force or dependency. Act according to your nature – these are the teachings of Yoga in Daily Life®.

It is beneficial to support a natural and free development of the personality from early childhood. But, instead, children are made fearful of sinfulness and the threat of God's punishment. There is pressure on the psyche as a result of this, which many people cannot overcome even as adults.

Even if a person only owns a dry piece of bread, but is inwardly free, he is a much happier person than someone who receives butter and cheese but has to live in dependency.

Be free, free of everything.

> *A king put this question to a Yogi, "Swamiji, how come people congregate around you in such numbers? You are poor like a beggar and own nothing you could give them. How come all these people, including myself, are still drawn to you over and over again?"*
> *The Yogi answered, "Because you are the slave of my slave."*
> *Surprised, the King asked," Don't you recognise me? I am no servant. I am the king of this country!"*
> *"I know very well who you are," said the Yogi. "Even so, I still maintain that you are the slave of my slave."*
> *The king did not understand this reply and demanded, "So tell me, which slave am I serving according to you."*
> *The Yogi answered, "Mind is my slave. But you are the slave of your mind, that is why you come to me."*

As long as we are slaves to our mind and senses, we will always be unhappy. Mind and senses should be our servants, working for us, while we are meditating on God.

To be happy means to be free emotionally and mentally. Being together with the Master gives us this freedom. Nothing is more precious in this life than to be free.

Even though we know what freedom means, we do not live freely.

Starting from today, follow the principles of Yoga in Daily Life®: that is how you will make your freedom reality. If everyone would do this, we could create paradise on this planet. Think positively and practice your *mantra*; this is a meaningful contribution to a better world.

Why do you think badly of someone? Why not think well of them instead? Good and bad, God and devil only exist in your own mind. Examine your inner world: if there is harmony, you will also find harmony in the outer world.

Be content! Be grateful for what you have, and be certain that everything that is meant to be yours will come to you.

I understand each one of you. I love you all and you love me. For many people this is inconceivable.

Our relationship does not mean dependency, but the opposite. It means freedom.

I do not make any material demands upon you. I only wish that you could let go of your jealousy and think freely. I wish that you would honour the right to life of all beings, and love all.

I pray daily that all people who come to me will be free of all *karmas* and reach God-realisation. This I wish for me and for you.

I also need your blessing, your love, your light, your under-standing and support. Between us a continuous river of giving and receiving flows.

Be free forever. Realise freedom in your daily life. When you succeed in this, you will have achieved something very beautiful. Do whatever you wish, but do it in freedom. This is the birth right given to you by God.

Always remember: whatever you are doing, in the end you are doing it for yourself. Whatever you are giving, you will get it back twofold. When you do good, you will receive twice as much in return. If you do bad, this will also come back to you doubled.

There is a story about this:

A man prayed to God day and night to be rich.
Finally, God appeared in front of him and asked: "What is it you wish for?"
The man answers, "A siddhi."
"Which siddhi?"
"I wish that everything I touch will become gold."
God granted the Siddhi to the man and he went home happy.
He was hungry and wanted to eat something, but as soon as he touched the food it turned into gold. He wanted to drink, but as soon as the water came close to his lips it turned into gold. In desperation he called for his wife. When she entered the room with their children he forgot himself and ran towards them to hug them. Immediately, they froze into golden statutes.
He now understood what a curse he had put on himself with his thoughtless wish. He ran as quickly as he could

into the forest and prayed to God from the bottom of his heart to appear once more before him.

After a while God appeared and asked, "Do you have enough gold now or do you wish for some more?"

Wringing his hands the man cried, "Lord, I beg you, take this terrible siddhi from me and bring my wife and children back to life! But if you do wish to give me something I ask only for one thing, grant me bhakti. Grant me love and devotion to all living beings."

And God blessed him and spoke, "It will be as you wish."

Whatever you ask for you will receive, and it will be even more than you can imagine. Firstly, carefully consider what it is you wish for and if it is truly important to you and your life.

You can only take out of your pocket what is in there. Only what is within your consciousness can reveal itself. It shows itself in your words, your deeds and your thoughts. Strive to fill your consciousness with contents that are beautiful and positive.

Think generously, think freely, think with love, think clearly and think Divine. Be joyful and without fear. This is what will make you Divine.

Be Content

Be content with what you have.

Practice both your *mantra* and Yoga in Daily Life® , and then you will experience enlightenment.

Do not pray for new techniques and *kriyas*.

If a child asks his parents for something, they will only fulfil his wish if they know that it is good for the child. Similarly, I will only give another *kriya* if I can see that the spiritual vibration of the disciple is ready for it.

Most importantly, follow the path you have started with confidence, and practise in the way I have told you. The protection and teaching of Mahaprabhuji is immense, so trust in Him completely.

A Yogi has no expectations, because he knows that expectations always end in disappointments. When there is expectation, there is also personal interest and selfish desire, whereas Yoga leads to universal consciousness.

A few years ago, two men came to me and asked for a *mantra*. A year later they came back, annoyed that they had not yet achieved miraculous powers through the *mantra*. They demanded a new *mantra* that would grant them supernatural powers.

I told them, "Why do you want such powers? This only proves that you wish to go against the Divine principle. In this way you will never achieve *siddhis*. While working against God you will destroy yourself."

A Rakshasa (demon) meditated day and night to achieve a certain siddhi. After a long time of strict asceticism and practices Lord Shiva finally appeared to him and granted him the fulfilment of a wish. The demon replied, "I wish for the siddhi that anyone whose head I touch with my hand will burn immediately."

In this story Lord Shiva symbolises our innocence, and the *Rakshasa* our greed.

The good-natured Shiva agreed and granted the demon this power. Triumphantly, the Rakshasa cried scornfully: "Thank you Lord Shiva! You will be the first one I try my new power out on!" With these words he stepped towards Lord Shiva. Of course, Shiva escaped, but the demon followed him. In his desperation, Shiva sought refuge with Lord Vishnu and asked him for help.

Vishnu symbolises our *VIVEKA*; our intelligence and power of discernment. *Viveka* often has to decide wisely and quickly in order to save us.

Reassuringly, Lord Vishnu spoke to Shiva: "Do not worry, all will turn out well. Just follow my advice. Transform yourself into a beautiful woman who will turn the head of the Rakshasa. Once he has totally fallen for you, then show him how to dance. Tell him to imitate all your movements exactly. Then when you casually touch your head with your hand, he will burn himself while imitating you."

Shiva did exactly as Vishnu suggested. He took the form of a beautiful dancer and appeared on the path the demon had taken in his pursuit. Totally enchanted with this Maya, the demon was easily persuaded to give up his hunt for Shiva and dance with this beauty instead. With

full concentration he imitated all her movements. When she finally put her hand on her head, he thoughtlessly did the same. And so, he destroyed himself.
In this way Shiva was saved.

If you ask for a certain power, it could be that you are indirectly or unconsciously asking for your own destruction. For this reason, stay where you are and be content with what you have.

Pray to God:

"Lord, please protect me from arrogance, greed, ego and ignorance. Remove the clouds of my bad qualities. I do not ask any siddhis from you. All I want is to serve you. Grant me only Bhakti. Grant me your love."

This is the best and most certain path to God.

All will come to you when the time is ripe.

Practise makes a master.

Yoga is a system that has not changed since its origin thousands of years ago. It is a path for all people. Yoga is the way back to your source. Anyone who recognises what Yoga means for all of humanity is blessed and happy. You have already recognised this, so now it is important that you continue to practise consistently.

In Europe it is said, *"All beginnings are difficult."*

However, I am of the opinion that: *"To start is not too difficult, but to continue and see it through is difficult."*

Protect Yourself

On a cold and rainy day, a bird sat in his warm nest on a tree, enjoying his protected and comfortable home. Then he saw a monkey completely wet and trembling with cold at the bottom of the tree,
Filled with pity, the little bird wanted to help the monkey with some good advice and said to him, "Why don't you build yourself a nest like mine and you won't have to freeze anymore!"
Annoyed, the monkey looked up the bird, thinking, "Who does this guy think he is, giving me advice? I know what I have to do for myself!" Furiousl,y he climbed up the tree and destroyed the bird's nest.

In *Kali Yuga*, the age in which we live now, the greater part of humanity is out of harmony with nature. Many cruel, nonsensical deeds are the result of this. For this reason, it is advisable to think carefully before you tell somebody something or give them advice. Pray you don't lose track of your path, and allow others to act according to their own decisions.

In *Kali Yuga* it is essential to protect yourself. The clouds of ignorance are very dense and widely spread, but one day the sun of wisdom will shine again.

Self-protection also means to be constantly attentive and conscious.

A prince was initiated as a Swami by his Master, Mahavir. A few days after his initiation, the prince wanted to know

what his task would be now and asked his Master about it.
The Master replied, "Continue to do everything you have done up until now: work, eat, pray, sleep and practice."
The prince was very surprised and asked, "And how will this be the different from my life before the initiation?"
"The only difference is that you will now do everything consciously."

Initiation means the awakening of consciousness. To act consciously is a very important self-protection. Awareness costs you nothing; but carelessness may even cost you your life.

Self-protection also consists of avoiding bad company and malevolent gossip.

The greatest danger on our path is *Maya*, which appears to us in the form of temptation in many shapes and forms.

How can you protect yourself from *Maya*?

Once she is already there, it is too late. Then only your inner strength can help you to endure and not drift from your path through her influence. Essential aids are TITIKSHA (steadfastness) and SAMADHAN (goal orientation).

In a flood, many plants are pulled out and washed away. But those whose roots are anchored deeply in the ground cannot be washed away. For this reason, anchor your roots deeply in God, so the flood of *Maya* cannot distract you from your path.

Ask your Master to help you, as Holy Guruji prays to Mahaprabhuji in his *bhajan*:

SRI DIPA DAYALU ARAJA SUNA LIJO

Hear my request, Merciful Mahaprabhuji!
Lead me to Satsang.
Protect me from those people who have a bad
influence upon me.
May my meditations always be directed
towards the Supreme.
Make my vairagya strong and constant,
So that nothing can distract my mind.
Don't let me fall into the errors of Maya!

Mahaprabhuji will always protect you, but you should still always work on yourself. Endeavour to be strong, have clarity and purity!

Holy Women

QUEEN CHUDALA

King Shikhardas, a just and peace-loving ruler, had a very intelligent, loving and spiritual wife.

One day, the king was forced to defend his country against an enemy attack. In the middle of the battlefield, when faced with the horrific sight of violence of death, he suddenly became aware of the cruelty and senselessness of war.

This recognition caused him to experience deep *vairagya*. He could only see disappointment, suffering and torture throughout the whole world, and felt a great longing for God. He left the battlefield immediately, and, without being seen, escaped to the seclusion of the Himalayas. There, he built himself a small hut and spent the whole day in spiritual practice and meditation.

His wife was deeply disturbed by his sudden disappearance. She sent out several men to search for him, but they found no trace. The Queen then decided to apply a more unusual method. She wanted to search for her husband in her meditation via astral travelling. She went to a spiritual Master and asked him to give her a *mantra* and spiritual practices that would result in her attaining this skill. The Queen used these practices in her meditation and practised continuously, day and night.

After several years of hard discipline and practice, the Queen finally achieved Self-realisation. Now she was able to leave her body at will and move to any chosen destination in this world via astral travel. Finally, after many months of tenacious searching, she discovered the king in his hideaway in the Himalayas. She saw him meditating and realised immediately that he was still in deep ignorance and far away from Self-realisation. He had practised without the guidance of a Master and was lacking the blessing of the *Guru-mantra*.

As a result of her spiritual Sadhana, the Queen was able to change her form at will. Knowing that her husband would never change his mind because of the sentimental words of his wife, she chose to appear in front of the king in the form of a venerable *Rishi*.

The King rose in order to greet the *Rishi* in the proper way. The wise man said to him: "I am Kumbha Rishi and am on my way to *Vaikuntha* to visit to the gods. I have been observing your meditation for some time. I can see that you are lacking the guidance of a realised Master. Without this guidance you will not be successful. If you wish, however, I will help you. I will give you a *mantra* and teach you certain practices through which you will reach your goal."

Filled with the gratitude the king received the teachings of the supposed *Rishi*. After his *mantra* initiation the *Rishi* left again, but not without the promise to return again after some time.

Overjoyed that she had finally found her husband again, the Queen returned to her palace. From then on, she frequently visited the king in the form of Kumbha Rishi and gave him *satsang* regularly.

After some time had passed she told him, "You will not be able to reach your goal in this place, because you still need to fulfil your duties in the world. You need to return to your home, your family and your people. I give you the unbreak-able promise that you will achieve Self-realisation through the fulfilment of your *dharma* in your palace."

The King was reluctant to return, but bowed to the advice of his Master. Before he left he asked his Master to grant a blessing to always appear to him whenever he called for him in prayer. The *Rishi* granted him his wish.

When the King returned to his palace he was joyfully received by everyone except the Queen who appeared to be hurt and withdrawn. The King asked humbly for her forgiveness for his flight and explained his reasons. He also spoke about his Master enthusiastically. The Queen said, "I would like to get to know this Master." The King replied joyfully, "This shall happen at once, because my Master promised that he would appear to me whenever I asked Him."

Smiling the Queen stood up and, in front of her astounded husband, took on the form of the Kumbha Rishi. A deep love vibrated in her voice when she announced told him, "It was me who came to you in the Himalayas and gave you your *mantra*. With the grace of my Master and through my love for you I achieved Self-realisation. In this way I was able to help you on your path with my knowledge. Now it is certain that you too will achieve your goal through your own practice."

SANGAMITRA

It is said about the Indian Emperor Ashok that his empire was so vast that the sun would not go down over it. The wheel that is used as a symbol on the Indian flag is named after this emperor. The Ashok wheel is nothing other than the "wheel of birth and rebirth." Its second meaning is the "wheel of time".

Ashok was a disciple of the Buddha, and it had become his life goal to spread the holy teachings throughout the entire country.

The emperor had a daughter named Sangamitra, who loved him above all else. As he was lying on his deathbed she faithfully stood by his side. The girl knew that his leaving the world was imminent, but could feel that some worry was keeping him from leaving.

"Father what is wrong?" she implored him. "What attachment is still there? Why don't you free yourself from all the worldly worries and dissolve into the eternal, blissful Light?

The father pointed at all the relatives, dignitaries and ministers surrounding his bed and replied, "I know for certain that only my worldly inheritance is of interest to all those present. But who would be suited to continue the spiritual legacy given to me by my Master, whom I faithfully served throughout my whole life?"

Sangamitra answered him: "Father, I give you my sacred vow that I will pass on these teachings."

Her father asked her to consider that it would be difficult for a woman to walk such a path and to take on such a big responsibility. But she was tenacious and insisted on her vow. Finally, the emperor gave her his blessings and left his mortal form.

From then on, Sangamitra lived the life of a *Sant* (saint), using all her energy to spread the teachings of the Buddha to the people. She held *satsang*s and gave countless lectures. Many listeners gathered around her, but in the end she could not convince them, no matter how urgently she presented the teachings.

One day, Sangamitra asked a few trusted friends why no one would seriously follow what she gave to the people in her many lectures and *satsangs*. She was told that the majority of visitors did not come to her due to their spiritual interest but were drawn to see her for the sake of her physical beauty. This realisation saddened her deeply. She thought, "If my impermanent outer beauty is an obstacle for people on their path to find the permanent truth, what use is it?"

Bearing in mind the vow that she had given to her father on his deathbed, she poured strong acid over her face and destroyed the loveliness of her features. At the same time, her inner beauty grew to such a degree that people were attracted by the divine light now radiating from her, unhampered by her outer glamour. Her words opened the hearts of thousands of people and spread the teachings of Buddha through many areas in the world.

MEERA

Meera was also the daughter of a King. One day, when she was five years old, she observed a wedding parade passing by the palace. Deeply impressed with the brilliant glamour of the festive parade she pressed her mother: "I also want to marry. Please tell me who will be my husband?" The mother tried to put her off till later. But the girl kept on begging, "Mother please tell me who is my husband!" Then the mother jokingly replied, "Lord Krishna is your husband."

Meera took her words completely seriously. From then on, no one else but Krishna was her destined spouse. Therefore, she was even more desolate when at the age of nineteen, she was married to a foreign king according to custom.

But this did not change her mind at all. To the great displeasure of her husband and his whole family, she continued to stay faithful to her beloved Lord Krishna in her thoughts, words and in everything she did.

Her spiritual Master, a Self-realised divine soul whom she visited daily, was a simple man – a common shoemaker. The royal family, whose judgmental and limited thinking regarded the relationship as scandalous, tried everything to get Meera away from him. When all attempts failed, they finally decided to kill Meera. They put poison in a cup and gave it to her to drink under the pretence it was holy water sent by her Master. Without hesitating for one second Meera emptied the cup and sang, without being affected at all by the poison, a *bhajan* to the honour of her Master.

MOYE LAGI LAGANA *GURU* CARANANA KI
CARANA BINA MOYE KACHU NAHI BHAVE
JAGA MAYA SABA SAPANANA KI
BHAVA SAGARA SABA SUKHA GAYO HE
PIKAR NAHI MOHI TRANANA KI
MEERA KE PRABHU GIRIDHARA NAGARA
ASA VAHI *GURU* CARANANA KI

The fire of my longing to be at the lotus
feet of my Master burns within me,
To transverse the ocean of Maya.
My longing will only stop at his lotus feet.
The world with her false glamour is only
a passing dream.
The ocean of the world holds no
terror for me anymore.
It lies dry before me
My only hope in this world is
directed to my Gurudev!"

The family tried another attempt on her life, and hid a poisonous snake in a basket. They gave it to Meera with the pretence that a statue of Krishna was inside. When Meera opened the basket, she found a well-crafted golden chain.

The King in particular was angry that Meera left the palace every evening at prayer time to go and visit the temple. In his jealousy, he suspected his wife of meeting with a lover. He posted guards everywhere with the instruction to report any suspicious circumstances to him immediately.

One night the guards heard voices in Meera's bedroom. They immediately went to wake the King who angrily rushed into her bedroom, with a sword in hand. He only found Meera, by herself, sitting on her bed with a transfigured look on her face.

"With whom are you talking?" the King demanded to know.
"With Krishna," Meera answered.
"Where is he? I cannot see him!" said the King, looking helplessly around the room.
"Of course, you cannot see Him with your physical eyes. For this you have to use different eyes," came Meera's reply.

In his rage the King raised his sword in order to kill Meera. But she stayed completely calm under his threat. She had become a Jivanmukta, a liberated soul who had no more fear. As the King directed his sword towards her, he suddenly saw four figures in front of him who all looked like Meera. At the same time, he heard a thunderous voice warning him, "Be careful, King, you can only kill the real Meera! If you miss her, you yourself will die." The King was horrified, dropped his sword and ran out of the room.

Soon after that, Meera left her home and travelled across India. During this time, she experienced Krishna in many apparitions and visions, describing these events in her deeply moving *bhajans*. Once when she was singing another song to express the love in her soul to Krishna, a man stopped in front of her. "Through your song resounds the voice of God." He gave her a small string instrument that from that moment she always carried with her.

After her travels, Meera returned to her hometown. But it did not take long until another attack was directed against her. Paid plaintiffs accused her in front of the *Brahmans* of having broken the religious rules. A tribunal of priests condemned her to death by poison. While putting the cup to her lips she prayed to God to forgive those who were responsible for her death.

Just as before, the poison had no effect on her. The opposite occurred and she started to dance and sing in ecstasy, "If I had known that love is so painful, I would not have fallen in love."

As she sang, Meera walked towards the Krishna temple. A big crowd followed her, curious to see when the poison would finally show its deadly effect. In the temple Meera bowed in front of Krishna's statue. In front of all these people she dissolved into light and forever became one with her beloved Lord.

Nowadays, Meera is worshipped in India and the whole world as a great Saint. A shining star of love, to the faithful she represents the embodiment of devotion and love for God, known as *Bhakti*.

The spiritual path can be quite hard in some ways, but also very beautiful. Unshakable trust and unconditional love forms its foundation. Spirituality is not possible without love. No one who has started on the path out of love for God has had an easy life. You only have to think of the sufferings of Jesus. But love, pure love, is stronger than any emotion.

Love knows no obstacles, neither in this or any other world.

Whatever happens to us, be it happiness or suffering, we need to recognise it as a sign on the path to lead us further. First of all, it is necessary that we overcome the ego, doubts and complexes until we finally discover the endless source of love within us. From this we can find the strength to endure all difficulties on the path, until we finally unite with the divine light of love.

Two Candles

Health, harmony and union lead to a healthy world. In order to achieve this, it is first necessary to work on ourselves.

One basic step is to become independent. We need to aim at depending on nothing, not even our own body. Our body should be under our control, not the other way round. Physical, mental, social and spiritual independence are of fundamental significance for the development of human consciousness.

Only an independent consciousness can develop and flower. The flowers of consciousness are: love, harmony, tolerance, understanding, contentment, peace, and union with nature and with God. The essence and fruit of this flowering is God-realisation. This means the recognition that God is omniscient and omnipresent.

We are all children of *one* father, creatures of *one* creator. *One* creator is the origin of all living beings. We need not only to accept this fact theoretically, but also experience it internally and put it into practice.

Tons of theory means nothing compared to a gram of practice.

Now is the time that people turn to Yoga. Yoga is the fundamental cosmic principle that unifies all elements of life. With this principle, harmony is created and preserved between the planets and cosmic forces, between the forces of nature and the cosmic laws. Yoga is the science of body, mind, consciousness and soul.

To realise this, we need to practise. To practise Yoga, no outer tools are required. All you need is effort and willpower.

Your practice should not be determined by thoughts or emotions. We need to be the master of our feelings and senses, of our body and mind. They should be our slaves, not the other way around. A human being that is a slave to his senses, mind and feelings is suffering more than any animal.

Human beings are the most suffering, the most discontent and most frequently sick creatures on this planet. What is the reason for this? The cause lies in the fact that humans disregard the laws of nature and become the slaves of their senses.

Try to understand and recognise yourself. Maintain your discipline and watch your senses, thoughts and feelings. That is Yoga in Daily Life®.

Nobody will come to you and give you liberation. You will have to work for it yourself.

Enlightenment, liberation, wisdom and God-realisation are very beautiful words. They are empty if you have not experienced them for yourself.

Knowledge is infinite and has no limits. Knowledge is gained through practice and experience. However, in every area of life you will need a Master to learn. To gain spiritual knowledge you need a spiritual Master.

Master and disciple are like two candles: one candle is burning, and the other one is not yet lit.

The fact that the other candle is not burning does not mean that it is incapable of giving light, only that it is not yet alight.

The Master is the burning candle and the disciple is the other. For the candle of the disciple to be well lit, they have to come close to the Master. This means the disciple has to follow the words of the Master and learn.

The disciple should not do as the Master does, but as the Master says. Such a disciple will become enlightened. He will become a Master himself.

The life of such a disciple will be happy in all respects: family, profession and free time. There will be happiness and joy in all aspects of their life.

Even though we know what it means to be happy and no one stops us from being so, still we are mostly unhappy.

Why is this? It is because we depend on external circumstances. But we cannot expect joy from the outer world. It arises from our inner attitude, through our inner contentment.

Yoga in Daily Life® is the path that will lead us to contentment, harmony, joy, peace, understanding, love, and, finally, to God-realisation.

Wedding Ceremony

To find a life partner and lifelong friend is a great blessing.

The souls of the man and woman are now one. Their bodies are like the wings of a bird flying towards the sky.

Now the most important duty for both of you is to go together through all the difficulties that life presents you with. You should live together in harmony and trust, and never quarrel. You should share happiness and unhappiness and stay together forever. Whatever belongs to one of you will also belong to the other.

I wish for you the blessings of Mahaprabhuji. May you both walk together, hand in hand, on the Divine path towards His Kingdom. I wish you many happy hours in your life and bless you with this *mantra*:

OM SUBHAM KAROTI KALYANAM
AROGYAM DHANSAMPADAH
SATRU*BUDDHI*-VINASAYA
DIPAJYOTIR-NAMOASTU TE

Lord give us joy and liberate us.
Give us health and harmony and protect us
from all negativity.
You are the wisdom and the light.
We bow to your Divine light, please shine
your light on our path.

I wish you harmony in all the three Tapas: *Adhi-Bhautika, Adhi-Daivika* and *Adhi-Atmika.* For your protection I will sing the MAHA MRITYU JAYA *MANTRA* three times:

OM TRYAMBAKAM YAJAMAHE
SUGANDHIM PUSTIVARDANAM
URVA RUKAMIEVA BANDHANAT
MRITYOR MUKSHIR MA AMRITAT
OM SHANTIH SHANTIH SHANTIH

We worship the three-eyed God, who is everywhere and protects all living beings.
May He save us from death and lead us to immortality.
OM – *Peace Peace Peace.*

According to Vedic tradition, both promise to accept the other as partners. The woman demonstrates her agreement as she hangs a flower *mala* around the neck of her husband. In turn, he does the same to her.

Flowers symbolise love, harmony and luck. The flower petals symbolise wealth, joy and growth of the family. The *mala* symbolises their union.

This is a special moment for both of you. I ask all of you present to wish them best wishes in your thoughts and to stand beside them.

Together the couple now takes a third flower *mala* and puts it on the altar.

I bless you both and wish you a happy life, much love, harmony and God's blessings.

Kindle my heart's flame with thine flame,
Sataguru kindle my heart's flame with thine

May thy light banish darkness forever
Sataguru kindle my heart's flame with thine

Oh Lord of Yoga, Lord of all wisdom
Oh Lord within all, Oh Lord above all
Shower Thy grace on Thy children
Sataguru kindle my heart's flame with Thine

May Thy light banish darkness forever
Sataguru kindle my heart's flame with Thine.

Lord we Thy children seek Thee at Thy gateway
Appear in Thy glory before us
Sataguru kindle my heart's flame with Thine.

May Thy light banish darkness forever
Sataguru kindle my heart's flame with Thine.

It's Thee whom we worship praying for Thy mercy
Love's nectar shower upon us
Sataguru kindle my heart's flame with Thine.

May Thy light banish darkness forever
Sataguru kindle my heart's flame with Thine.

For ages within us that power has been slumbering
Awaken Chit Shakti within us
Sataguru kindle my heart's flame with Thine

May Thy light banish darkness forever
Sataguru kindle my heart's flame with Thine.

For long in our hearts that ember has been smouldering
To the music of So Ham awake us
Sataguru kindle my heart's flame with Thine

May Thy light banish darkness forever
Sataguru kindle my heart's flame with Thine.

Immortal soul of my Gurudeva
Our lives at Thy feet we surrender
Sataguru kindle my heart's flame with Thine

May Thy light banish darkness forever
Sataguru kindle my heart's flame with Thine.
Kindle my hearts flame with Thine flame
Sataguru kindle my heart's flame with Thine

Stay with your decision

Sometimes in life we need to make a decision quickly, and sometimes it is best to wait.

Don't hesitate when you are making decisions regarding good things. For bad things, you can't wait long enough...

Spiritually it is best to decide on *one* path after you have thought about it carefully, and then follow this path for the rest of your life. God will always support us on our path. Where there is a will, there is a way.

Think carefully about your decision and stick to whatever agreements you have made with yourself without wavering. Many of you have made a promise to me, an inner promise deep within your hearts. Always be conscious of this promise, and one day it will become reality.

You and I know of your deep desire for devotion, for God, and for Self-realisation. You have been through much in making this decision. Stick to it. Mahaprabhuji is always with us and will help us.

Some of you would like to become a *Swami* (monk). I respect this desire and will think it over. However, you need to realise what awaits you as a *Swami*.

The life of a *Swami* is not as easy as some of you may think. To live as a *Swami* means to continuously go through the fire, the fire of purification.

To be a *Swami* means to be a Hindu monk. It is not so easy for a Hindu monk to live in the Western culture. You are dependent on many outer circumstances and that is not always comfortable.

When someone makes the decision to become a *Swami*, it is down to the work of many lives, and a real blessing from God.

A Swami has to be ready to sacrifice a lot. He or she has to sacrifice the ego and all personal feelings. "I like this, I don't like this...", this way of thinking has to be removed by its roots. All attachment to the family, individual people or material things also has to be overcome, because a *Swami* dedicates his life to all people. As it says in this poem:

> *I am like the wind, no one can hold me back.*
> *I am like the sky, no one can own me;*
> *I don't belong to anyone*

To reach to the first step of being a *Swami*, it takes twelve years. During this time the disciple should live the life of a BRAHMACHARYA, an aspirant who follows the discipline given to him by His Master. He dedicates all this time to the study of spiritual knowledge.

One does not become a *Swami* only through your own will or because someone else chooses you. One becomes a *Swami* solely through the development of the necessary qualities.

First you have to develop into being a *Swami*. Become a pure flame of the Divine, and then everything else will simply come to you. As long as there is no light, the moths will not come. As soon as the sun rises however, everyone will know it immediately and say joyfully, *"Look, the sun is up!"*

Gurupurnima

Today we celebrate the memorable day on which every disciple directs his thoughts with special devotion and love to his Master, his *GURU*.

GU means darkness, and *RU* means light. *GURUPURNIMA* is the day on which the light of the sun touched our planet for the first time. *Gurupurnima* is the day on which the known part of the cosmos was illuminated for the first time.

But the real source of light is not the sun. The sun only reflects the splendour of the divine light, the divine power and energy that makes her shine.

Life began on planet Earth with the light of the sun. Human life started much later; but life as a manifestation (as opposed to the non-manifest, the "non-being") began at this point.

All life requires love; it requires a perfectly pure love. This life-giving love flows to us as *PRAKRITI* (nature) in the form of the rays of the moon, and as *PURUSHA* (consciousness) in the form of sunlight.

MOHA, the force of attraction between opposites, affects *prakriti* and *purusha*. Creative will and the longing to create originate from *moha*. As these three principles began to work, a fourth principle, *AHAMKARA*, the ego, developed. In this context, "Ego" means individuality, or the will to live, in the sense of: "*I* wish to exist." This "I" was the seed that multiplied itself and from which thousands of seeds spread. All these were just like the seeds of one tree, all of the same kind.

Where there is life, there is light, regardless of it is life in the physical or astral form. Where light exists, there is also darkness. The whole cosmos is filled with light and darkness. On full moon day, however, and especially on *Gurupurnima*, we praise the light.

About seven thousand years ago there lived a great Saint, MAHARISHI VYASA. He was the author of the great epic the MAHABHARATA. He also recorded the holy *Vedas*. For this reason, he is also called VED VYASA. VEDA means knowledge. Knowledge is light. Light is GURU. The consciousness of Ved Vyasa was spotlessly pure and totally enlightened. Not the slightest seed of ignorance existed within him.

Gurupurnima is the birthday of Ved Vyasa; that is why this day is also called *VYASA PURNIMA*.

Gurupurnima is the highest spiritual day that can be celebrated in this universe. Happy and blessed are those disciples who can be with their Master on this day, and those who are with their Master in thought receive His blessings.

Today we stand at the beginning of a new spiritual year. Make a special prayer today for the blessings of your *Satguru* and for His help to progress further on your spiritual path. Make a new *SANKALPA* to practise even more intensely and to develop even more *bhakti* from now on.

Without the understanding of the *GURU PRINCIPLE* and the meaning of life, light and love you will miss the true purpose of your life and your spiritual path.

The disciple symbolises the earth, and the Master the sun. The first meeting between Master and disciple results in the disciple receiving their first glimpse of the light of knowledge within him or her. With the grace of the Master, His *MANTRAS*, His blessing and His whole being, the Master kindles the Divine spark in the heart of the disciple.

It is now the duty of the disciple to care for and protect this light of life through *BHAKTI*, *VAIRAGYA*, *GYANA* and *ABHYASA*.

Without *bhakti,* spiritual life is not possible. Without *vairagya,* the path quickly ends in the jungle of dependence and greed. Without *gyana,* the light extinguishes, and without *abhyasa,* the seed sown by the master into the heart of the disciple will dry up.

It is important that the disciple understands the Master and realises the true purpose of life. For some people, several lifetimes are necessary to comprehend this. To just be born as human is not enough; it is also necessary to develop compassion and love for all living beings. The true human qualities will only develop in the person through this.

Whoever truly understands the quality of *bhakti* will also understand the true meaning of *Guru*. With *bhakti,* there is no distance. Without *bhakti,* even the door of your neighbour may create too great a distance for you to meet each other. It is significant not only where your physical body is, but also where you direct your thoughts.

I pray to Sri Devpuriji, Mahaprabhuji and Holy Guruji for your good health, harmony, good fortune and spiritual development. May our Masters protect us and lead us further on our path.

Kindle the light of *Gurudeva* in your heart, feel it shine, and take special care that it is never extinguished again.

Sri Devpuriji

The Siddha Dhuni, or Siddha Dham Ashram is situatated in the Himalayas between the places of pilgrimage, Kedarnath and Badrinath (Himachal Pradesh). Here, Sri Alakh Puriji, the Master of Sri Devpuriji, occasionally spends some time with a few disciples. He is one of the great *SIDDHAS*, or *RISHIS*, of *SATYA LOKA*, the highest cosmic plane of truth and reality.

The seven *Rishis* are protectors of this world and sometimes visit the earthly plane in their physical form, but mostly they remain invisible. Their true age is unknown to us; however, they have been living for thousands of years. They are capable of rejuvenating their bodies and changing their shape at will, as they live beyond the conditions of the material world. Like Sri Devpuriji, the legendary Babaji is also one of these great Yogis.

Sri Devpuriji is an embodiment of Lord Shiva. Shiva is the liberator. He is the destroyer of whatever is bad and wicked. Shiva is consciousness, purity and fire. He protects his devotees.

Humanity owes the science of Yoga to Lord Shiva, who revealed this knowledge to his wife Parvati, and in doing so, gave Yoga to the whole world as a gift.

A *bhakta* who meditates on Lord Shiva will achieve liberation via the short route. Lord Shiva is the most benevolent and merciful of the Divine Trinity.

BRAHMA is the creator, *VISHNU* the preserver and *SHIVA*, or *MAHESH*, is the destroyer and liberator. These differences only exist because of what people are capable of imagining. These divine principles are aspects of the one reality, *VISHWA DEEP*, the one universal divine light. The "Three" are, in reality, "One".

When you are active and creative, *BRAHMA SHAKTI* is working within you. If you are helpful and friendly, you manifest *VISHNU SHAKTI*. Making clear decisions is possible through *SHIVA SHAKTI*.

In our world, the three gods are working in the form of the three *GUNAS*:

- *RAJAS GUNA* is *BRAHMA*,
- *SATTVA GUNA* is *VISHNU*,
- *TAMAS GUNA* is *SHIVA*.

The three *Gunas* maintain the equilibrium within nature. The *Gunas* create the cycle of becoming and dissolving, the cycle of death and rebirth.

Higher than the *Gunas* is the fourth principle of *GURU TATTVA*. In the principle of *Guru Tattva* the cycle of nature finishes. All movement comes to a standstill and all are unified in eternal bliss. This is why we say in our prayers, *"I bow to my Satguru, who stands above the three Gunas."*

Each of the three Divine manifestations has their own their own role to play in the universe. For this reason, humans make a great mistake if they choose to accept and honour only one of the aspects of God. Before the dissemination of Christianity, it was also believed in Europe that God manifested in many forms. People respected and revered God in nature by praying to the Sun God or the God of Water. This illustrates that people back then understood *SAT SANATAN DHARMA*. They understood their TRUE RELATIONSHIP TO GOD.

Whatever religion we belong to and whatever principles we live by, the universal principle always remains the same. The universal principle is the unchangeable reality. There are no powers through which we can influence the cosmic laws. They are the reality, not the different systems of thought through which different philosophies and religions originated.

For this reason, Yoga stands above all religions. Yoga was transmitted to humans by Lord Shiva and exists to this day without changes. The science of Yoga will never change. It is the pure unchangeable Truth.

> Once Arjuna had doubts about Lord Krishna and asked Him, "Master, how can I believe that you are the whole universe? Please show me your universal form."
> Lord Krishna answered, "It is not easy for a mortal being to endure this revelation, but since you asked me, I will fulfil your wish."
> With these words He changed His form and allowed Arjuna to see in Him all that has ever existed in this world; what exists today and what will exist in the future.
> Krishna revealed to Arjuna the good and the bad, the beautiful and the ugly, death and life; all the qualities and manifestations in His universal form.
> Soon Arjuna exclaimed, "Lord, I believe you, but please show yourself again in Your agreeable human form!"

All exists in God. The whole universe is as One and perfect. Our body is like a cosmos within a cosmos – a "micro-cosmos", so to speak. The whole universe is BRAHMAN and we are PINA, the physical universe.

To live according to the cosmic laws means to keep inner and outer harmony and balance. Make love, tolerance and recognition the principles that guide your life. To give freedom to others always means to be free yourself. Love your neighbour. Your neighbours are all living beings. Before God all are equal.

Sri Devpuriji

One day, when Srimati Chandandeviji, the Holy mother of Mahaprabhuji, was meditating, Lord Shiva came to her and promised to appear personally before her.

To fulfil this promise, Sri Devpuriji left the solitude of the Himalayas and went to Rajasthan. He could materialise himself at will in any space, at any time – even in several locations at once! This is only possible for God himself. Nothing is impossible for Sri Devpuriji. He has no limits.

Even His steps were so fine and light that he did not leave any footprints on the sand.
His Divine radiance filled the people who lived with him with a very special consciousness.

In Kailash *ashram,* Sri Devpuriji held many wonderful *satsang*s. Countless animals, including snakes, scorpions, dogs and birds, always surrounded him. He could talk to them because he understood and spoke the universal language. The animals sat and listened devoutly to his words. Many people also came to His *satsang*s, but mostly they were inattentive and talked among themselves. Hardly anyone followed His teachings seriously. Most people only paid attention to His words when they were having difficulties and needed help.

When Sri Devpuriji noticed that the people were not making spiritual progress, he stopped the *satsang*s.

During one *satsang* he suddenly shouted, "Quickly! Leave the room, the *ashram* will collapse!" At first, people doubted His words but finally, they did what He asked. No sooner had they left, than the upper storey of the *ashram* collapsed!

Then Sri Devpuriji called all His animals to Him and the people quickly ran from the hordes of snakes and scorpions ap-

179

proaching the *Ashram*. Most people believed that Sri Devpuriji had gone crazy, and hardly anyone understood the real reason for his behaviour.

From then on, Sri Devpuriji allowed only those who came with love and a pure heart to be close to Him.

The old part of the *ashram* remains unchanged to this day. A mighty tree towers through the roof and overshadows the fireplace where Sri Devpuriji meditated. From there, one has a beautiful, peaceful view over the land. The *ashram* of Kailash possesses a very strong, holy atmosphere, similar to what can be felt on the holy mountain of Kailash in the Himalayas, the place where Lord Shiva resides.

A man from Kailash reported this incredible and impressive miracle to me. He had been an eyewitness to this event when he was fourteen years old. He said,

> *"Sri Devpuriji had received an injury to His right calf that got worse and finally began to suppurate. The whole leg was inflamed and swollen.*
> *My father urged Sri Devpuriji to have a doctor treat the injury. But Sri Devpuriji only replied, "If the wound disturbs you I will simply cut it out."*
> *He took His sword and without hesitating cut all the flesh from the calf muscle to above the wound. Now the bones of half His leg lay bare. Then he took His turban and bound the open wound with the cloth. He then asked my father with a smile, "Do you like it better now?"*
> *My father and I watched His action, completely speechless. Soon after we said goodbye, still speechless with amazement and horror. We visited Sri Devpuriji the next day to see how He was. He showed us His leg, which was*

now completely healed. Not even the slightest trace of any injury or scar was visible."

The following story was reported to Holy Guruji by a former hunter:

"Once, when I had just put my kill of a few dozen birds in a basket, I saw Sri Devpuriji approaching me. Quickly, I hid the basket as I was afraid of Sri Devpuriji's anger."

When the wrath of Lord Shiva awakens, He opens His third eye and whatever He directs His glance toward will burn. For this reason, the first Laser ray was called "Shiva's eye."

"As Sri Devpuriji reached me he immediately asked,
"What have you hidden in the bushes?"
"Nothing, Master."
"Nothing?"
"Only something for my children," I finally stammered.
"You only think of your children but unfortunately not of the children of these birds," spoke the Master strictly. "Before God, nothing stays hidden. Hand me that basket immediately!"
When I passed Him the basket, He opened it, and what a miracle! All the dead birds simply flew away, awakened to a new life.
After this experience, I renounced the killing of animals forever."

We have the great fortune that whenever we travel to India, we can visit Kailash *ashram*, where we can absorb the atmosphere and energy of this holy place and offer our adoration and devotion to God.

Sri Devpuriji is God. He is the goal of all Yogis. He is our idol and our destination. For a long time, there was no picture or photo of Sri Devpuriji. Whenever someone asked him for a picture he said,

> "My picture is the sun. Whenever you
> wish to see me, look at the sun."

However, he allowed a few artists to paint a picture of him. So at least we have an image of His physical form.

Unfortunately, Sri Devpuriji's talks are not recorded, but I can pass on a few of His words to you.

- *"God takes upon himself the fate of His devotees."*
- *"Each thought, each word and each action that start with Gurudeva's blessings will certainly be successful."*
- *"There is no power in this universe that can hold you back in the long run. Keep Gurudev in your heart constantly and your success is certain."*

The words of Sri Devpuriji are the truth.

One day, Sri Devpuriji announced to His disciples that He was going to leave His physical body the next day to reunite with His cosmic light. People did not want to believe Him, as they saw Him sitting healthy and strong before them. However, the next day his words came true. Sri Devpuriji left his body during His meditation.

Later, a prayer hall was erected at this place.

In 1978, Sri Devpuriji appeared to Holy Guruji in his meditation. Overjoyed with His appearance, he greeted the divine Master with devotion. Sri Devpuriji smiled and spoke, *"I will now go to Mahesh in Europe. Deep is already there."* Holy Guruji was delighted with this news and reported it to me immediately in a letter that I have kept.

You are blessed to be the disciples of Sri Devpuriji. You have already been together with Mahaprabhuji and Sri Devpuriji in former lives. Never doubt, but rather have complete trust. Do not keep searching for something else since you have found everything already! Love God with all your heart and serve Him.

Not only you who are now sitting in this *Satsang*, but thousands – no, millions – of people will receive this message. Just now, the light is starting to awaken in their consciousness. Already it has started to grow and to spread.

All Yoga aspirants are under the protection of Sri Devpuriji. The science of Yoga in Daily Life® was conveyed to us by Sri Devpuriji and Mahaprabhuji. Sri Devpuriji will always protect us. He is always there when you think of Him and when you direct your adoration and love to Him. Meditate continuously on Sri Devpuriji.

My Path

Today I wish to tell you something of my time with Holy Guruji.

It was a very beautiful and, at the same time, very difficult time for me. Sometimes I would have liked to run away, however my love for Holy Guruji was far too strong.

I felt like the fox with the coconut: he would have liked to taste it, but could not open it. Constantly attracted by its sweet smell, he was unable to let it go.

Each of us decides on our path in life, and we should not deviate from this path.

I remember a movie that played in Russia. A group of men had to climb over a high mountain to reach the next valley. It happened to be deep winter, and it was icy cold with hurling snowstorms. The men suffered from hunger and were freezing. Some of them died, but the others did not give up. They continued on their difficult path to their goal.

In all these years that I have lived in Europe, I have noticed a great difference between Europe and India. In India, many more people try to be steadfast on their path. In Europe, however, people often change their path too flippantly and quickly.

But let's get back to my time with Holy Guruji. When I was thirteen I started living with him. After school I cleaned the Ashram, washed the laundry and prepared the meal.

Like every Master, Holy Guruji was hard sometimes and gentle at other times. There were occasions when I was happy that he went away travelling. However, as soon as he left, it appeared that all *prana* was drawn from me, and I only wished for him to come back soon.

The time with him was the most beautiful, but also the most difficult time in my life.

Most people run away from discipline. We don't like it when someone is strict with us. For this reason, sometimes I felt bad and other times I felt good.

To fetch the mail or complete some other duties for Holy Guruji, I had to travel up to forty kilometres on a bicycle. Often, I was glad to get away for a few hours. But the moments of returning to Holy Guruji were the most beautiful moments in my life.

I felt like a calf that is completely happy when it can drink its mother's milk and immediately starts to cry and lament when she moves away.

I went through hard training with Holy Guruji. A Master always wants the best for his disciple, just as the parents want the best for their children. Sometimes it is hard to comprehend the Master. It was the same for me; I did not always understand Holy Guruji. It was often not easy to live with him, but I would never have left him.

I stayed on the path that I had chosen. It is a character trait of mine that once I start something, I will carry on until its successful completion, for better or worse.

Some years later, I decided to become a *Swami*, and very soon after my initiation I left India to take the message of Mahaprabhuji to the whole world.

There is a story of a salt statue that wanted to know the depth of the ocean. She dived into the ocean and never came back. She had melted and dissolved into the ocean.

In this way, I too have melted into spirituality and have become one with Guruji's consciousness.

Today I know that everything Holy Guruji said and did was the right thing for me, and I am very grateful to him.

He is very deep in me and I am deep in him. We are two bodies but one soul.

Guruji's life was also often hard. Whoever dedicates his life to others has to renounce many things. The efforts and deprivations have left their mark on his physical body. When Guruji was young he had to walk a lot. He often carried twenty kilograms of books of Mahaprabhuji's *bhajans* in order to distribute them to the disciples.

Holy Guruji himself composed and sang many *bhajans* and opened the hearts of countless people to the light of Mahaprabhuji.

As Guruji's disciple, I see it as my duty to give him as much joy as I possibly can.

Even though Guruji and I are physically separated, we are inseparably one in all our sentiments.

When I make a telephone call to Holy Guruji, he often says, *"I have waited for your call like a dried-out field for rain."*

When a Master speaks such words to his disciple, it is very special and beautiful. I immediately forget all my difficulties and problems and feel one with him.

I always look forward to the moment when I can again see the form of my Master with my physical eyes. When we meet one another there are often tears of joy in Guruji's eyes. It is these moments that show his love. To cause tears in a person like Holy Guruji is not easy. He is beyond all, beyond emotions, beyond death, and beyond attachment. These feelings have nothing to do with attachment. These are feelings of love and joy. They overflow from the heart and become visible in the eyes, which are the mirror of the soul.

This is the Master, his eyes and his form. A touch from him is like a revelation.

Only those who have realised this can understand.

In life there are thousands of distractions and dangers for us; however, there are only a few opportunities and chances to experience God. Every day we are forced to make choices. Often it is not easy to know the difference between right and wrong, and each time it is a test for us.

No matter what confronts us, we should not simply decide with reason alone, but first consult our heart and always keep our goal in mind. In this way, we will purify all negative feelings, thoughts and doubts.

Practice brings mastery and without practice we will not move forward.

Yoga is our path. We have chosen it and now we pray for the strength to stay faithful to it and to move forward.

I pray to Mahaprabhuji that He will give me His blessing and His mercy to stay forever faithful to my Master.

My life shall be a joy to him.

Guruji knows that I care well for his disciples. To fulfil this task, I pray to Mahaprabhuji that he will always show me the right way, give me strength and lead me to the light.

This is my path. Wherever I am and wherever I go, my Master always lives in my consciousness and I am at one with Him.

"I am always with you!"

How is that possible?
When I am with you is the other one alone?
How is it possible to be everywhere at the same time?

This is Mahaprabhuji's answer to this question.

"The presence of the Master is like the sun or space."

Whether there are millions of people or only one, the sun shines for everyone. There is enough space for everybody. When you can see the Master in this way, you have understood.

We all breathe in oxygen. If one person takes a breath, does he then take the oxygen away from all the other people in this world? Do the others receive less oxygen because of his breath? No! Because there is enough for everybody, everyone can breathe as much oxygen as they want or need, and all at the same time.

Similarly, the Master is there for all His disciples, and each one of them receives what they need. Problems arise only when personal attachments start to develop.

We are all very dependent on the sun. We need the sun to survive. In this case it is a positive dependency, since no one wishes to own the sun for themself. But if people claimed the sunshine for themselves, excluding all others, they would certainly suffer.

Do not try to own the sun, but try and be like the sun yourself. Then you also will be able to be present with everyone at the same time.

Last week at a conference I heard some very true words spoken by a *Swami*: *"In life, joy and misery exist closely together at any one moment."*

If you feel joy, sorrow will certainly follow. If you are experiencing difficulties, you can be certain that happier days will come again.

Whoever can stay calm regardless of whether there is joy or sorrow has reached the state of ANANDA, blissfulness.

Only one who has transcended all dualism can achieve true blissfulness. Sorrow exists when the "I" is present.

We say, "I am." As long as the "I" is there, it will have to live through the contrasts of joy and sorrow, fortune and misery. When the "I" is overcome, there is only BE, BEING, IT IS.

Through your *mantra* and prayer try to always feel the Light of Mahaprabhuji and Sri Devpuriji's presence within you.

Through them, all of us are always and constantly connected with each other.

OM SRI DEEP NARAYAN BHAGWAN KI JAY!

Harmony for Body, Mind and Soul

www.yogaindailylife.org

www.swamiji.tv

www.youtube.com/yogaindailylife

www.facebook.com/VishwagurujiMaheshwaranandaji
www.facebook.com/www.yogaindailylife.org

www.instagram.com/yogaindailylife/

www.worldpeacecouncil.net

www.chakras.net

www.lilaamrit.org

www.omashram.com

www.helphospital.org

www.gyanputra.org

Printed in Great Britain
by Amazon

26977490R00116